"*Soar* offers a timely word for men looking to develop spiritual depth. I strongly encourage men everywhere to allow the guidance of the Holy Spirit, as outlined in this material, to lead them into a powerful, more meaningful relationship in Christ."

—BISHOP T. D. JAKES, founder and senior pastor, The Potter's House, Dallas

"In *Soar,* Kenny Luck tackles one of the greatest topics I believe the church needs to hear: the value of being surrendered fully to the lordship of Jesus Christ and to the leading of the Holy Spirit. It is only in living a life fully submitted and committed to God that we can be the reflection of His love and grace to others. And that's huge. I love this quote from *Soar:* 'The Holy Spirit is in you to change the way you think about everything.' I pray you will let God use this book to start making some of those changes."

—DINO RIZZO, lead pastor, Healing Place Church, Baton Rouge, LA,
    and author of *Servolution*

"Anytime you can get you can get your hands on a Kenny Luck book you're in for challenge and change. *Soar,* the latest addition to Kenny's series of masculine, streetwise theology, is no different. It's bold, unvarnished truth about the amazing person and work of the Holy Spirit. *Soar* gives a fresh perspective on how to understand and assess your relationship and connectedness to the Spirit so you really can enjoy your identity, legacy, and destiny in Christ."

—DAVE BROWN, director and pastor-at-large, Washington (DC) Area
    Coalition of Men's Ministries (WACMM)

Praise for Other Books in the God's Man Series

Risk

"Understanding the significance of the Christian message is of such great importance, there cannot be too many ways to bring it to our attention. *Risk* is certain to inspire readers who long to give their all to a mighty cause but who might miss the message if it were presented in a less passionate way."

—KEN BLANCHARD, co-author of *The One Minute Manager* and *The Secret*

"Shocking are Scripture's stories of men who took risks! So are the modern-day accounts of men changing the world for God by taking risks. And then there's you... Are you risking it? This is a man's book for men—men of God ready to rip into the ends of the age. Dive into *Risk*!"

—DR. WAYNE CORDEIRO, senior pastor, New Hope Christian Fellowship, Oahu, HI, and author of *Leading on Empty* and *Divine Mentor*

"I've always been an adrenaline junkie, so *Risk* instantly appealed to me. This book goes beyond the interesting and engaging descriptive stories to provide much-needed pre-scriptive insight to enable men to live more boldly and powerfully. If you're up for being challenged in significant ways, read this book."

—MARK SANBORN, president of Sanborn and Associates Inc. and author of *The Fred Factor* and *You Don't Need a Title to be a Leader*

Fight

"I felt like I was reading a Tom Clancy book on spiritual warfare. An enjoyable read on a deadly serious subject. You won't be disappointed."

—DAVID MURROW, author of *Why Men Hate Going to Church* and *The Map*

"I always want to know if the author of a book exemplifies what he has written. Kenny Luck certainly does!"

—TOM HOLLADAY, teaching pastor, Saddleback Church and author of *The Relationship Principles of Jesus*

"It's been said that all evil needs to succeed is for good men to do nothing. Kenny excels at showing the bigger story we're engaged in. *Fight* is a must-read for men to defeat the enemy where *each of us* live—in our marriages, our families, and all our spheres of influence."

—JIM WEIDMANN, "The Family Night Guy," executive director of Heritage Builders, and author of the Family Night Tool Chest series

soar

soar

Are you ready
to accept
God's POWER?

kenny luck

WATERBROOK
PRESS

Soar
Published by WaterBrook Press
12265 Oracle Boulevard, Suite 200
Colorado Springs, Colorado 80921

All scripture quotations, unless otherwise indicated, are taken from the Holy Bible, New International Version®. NIV®. Copyright © 1973, 1978, 1984 by Biblica Inc.™ Used by permission of Zondervan. All rights reserved worldwide. www.zondervan.com. Scripture quotations marked (ESV) are taken from The Holy Bible, English Standard Version, copyright © 2001 by Crossway Bibles, a division of Good News Publishers. Used by permission. All rights reserved. Scripture quotations marked (MSG) are taken from The Message by Eugene H. Peterson. Copyright © 1993, 1994, 1995, 1996, 2000, 2001, 2002. Used by permission of NavPress Publishing Group. All rights reserved. Scripture quotations marked (NASB) are taken from the New American Standard Bible®. © Copyright The Lockman Foundation 1960, 1962, 1963, 1968, 1971, 1972, 1973, 1975, 1977, 1995. Used by permission. (www.Lockman.org). Scripture quotations marked (NLT) are taken from the Holy Bible, New Living Translation, copyright © 1996, 2004. Used by permission of Tyndale House Publishers Inc., Wheaton, Illinois 60189. All rights reserved.

Italics in Scripture quotations reflect the author's added emphasis.

Details in some anecdotes and stories have been changed to protect the identities of the persons involved.

ISBN 978-1-57856-989-2
ISBN 978-0-307-44664-0 (electronic)

Published in the United States by WaterBrook Multnomah, an imprint of the Crown Publishing Group, a division of Random House Inc., New York.

WaterBrook and its deer colophon are registered trademarks of Random House Inc.

Library of Congress Cataloging-in-Publication Data
Luck, Kenneth L., 1964–
 Soar / Kenny Luck. — 1st ed.
  p. cm.
 Includes bibliographical references (p.   ) and index.
 ISBN 978-1-57856-989-2 (alk. paper) — ISBN 978-0-307-44664-0 (electronic : alk. paper)
 1. Christian men—Religious life. I. Title.
 BV4528.2.L86 2010
 248.8'42—dc22

                                    2010024535

Printed in the United States of America
2010—First Edition

10 9 8 7 6 5 4 3 2 1

Special Sales
Most WaterBrook Multnomah books are available at special quantity discounts when purchased in bulk by corporations, organizations, and special-interest groups. Custom imprinting or excerpting can also be done to fit special needs. For information, please e-mail SpecialMarkets@WaterBrookMultnomah.com or call 1-800-603-7051.

*This book is dedicated to my brothers and sisters standing bravely for Christ
before their persecutors by the power of the Holy Spirit.
You are soaring in the midst.*

contents

Part 3: Transactions

acknowledgments

Dr. Rick Warren, Dr. Bill Bright, Dr. Robert Morris, Dr. Kevin Springer, and so many others for blowing my mind with your learning posture, mentoring friendship, and commitment to the next spiritual revolution among men.

Part 1

transitions

in the midst

Hell on earth would be to meet the person you could have become.

—KEN BLANCHARD

"Don't fight me!"

The firm and calm rebuke came from Gary, a flight instructor with twenty-nine years of glider experience. Sailing along at four thousand feet above the ground over California's central coast, only moments before—after I had released the tow cable and Gary had trimmed us out—he asked, "Do you want to take the stick?"

"Yeah!" I yelled, almost bursting Gary's eardrum, and eagerly grabbed the stick with my whole hand. Unknown to me, Gary gripped his "chicken stick," which is the second flight control stick used by the instructor in case an overeager and undertrained novice forgets that flying gliders is not his day job.

Apparently, I had messed up, so Gary had rebuked me with his "Don't fight me!" command and took control of the aircraft.

Shocked and surprised at his words, I quickly released my hand from the stick.

"Let's try again," Gary said calmly. "Forward is down. Back is climb. Left is left, and right is right."

Slowly, I put my hand back on the stick and again grabbed it with my whole hand.

"Don't fight me!" Gary said even more firmly this time.

I felt the "invisible force" wiggle my hand off the stick. My spirits dived again after hearing those buzz-killing words: "Don't fight me." Patiently Gary explained one more time how less is more when you are riding the wind in a glider. Specifically, that means a thumb, an index finger, and light pressure on the stick. "Gently keep the nose up and head for that mountain," came the voice from behind me. "Gently," he repeated.

For the third time I assumed control, this time lightly grasping the stick with my thumb and index finger, and for the next fifteen exhilarating minutes I rode the wind. Gary told me where to fly the glider, and after each prompt, I gently leveraged the physics of those long, skinny wings to float us silently toward different points on the horizon. For me, the third try was the charm. It was amazing.

I got into a rhythm of small, calculated, subtle adjustments on the stick. The silence and lack of more chicken-stick takeovers from Gary meant that I had earned his confidence. I suppose embarrassment makes you listen more closely so that you apply instructions and integrate the learning pronto. For those fifteen "Don't fight me"–free minutes, the only gliding-related comments from Gary were of the chest-inflating nature. As in, "You're a natural."

When he said that, a loud voice in my brain shouted, What? Talk about a flip-flop! I've gone from "Don't fight me!" to "You're a natural" in ten minutes? What a turnaround!

I went from embarrassment to elation, from doghouse to penthouse, and from novice reactions and failure to a new intuition and success in the skies. High above the earth, inside that canopy, I was literally *and* emotionally soaring. Victory was snatched from the jaws of defeat, shame, and embarrassment. Selfishly, I was thinking what any man would be thinking: *Thank God, I turned it around up here!*

We landed, popped open the canopy, and were greeted by my buddy Paul, who asked, "How'd it go?"

Gary offered, "He's a natural."

Attaboy, Gary.

Now here's the embarrassing confession: I took that ride in the glider before writing this book, not to learn how to fly, but mainly to experience the feeling of soaring. I went up there for an emotional rush, not to get called out by a teacher! What a downer when all you want is to experience something, not to learn or think about it that much. I wasn't prepared for *correction.* But when Gary directed those three little words at me

> *What God wanted to tell me at this point in my life:* Don't fight Me.

four thousand feet above the ground, the real life lesson began to sink in. More specifically, a message from *up there* was being directed at me for consideration *down here* where I really live. Gary was the blissfully ignorant but perfect voice to say what needed to be said. Or rather, to say what God wanted to tell me at this point in my life: *Don't fight Me.*

Needle Sticks and Splinters

When someone says to another person, "Don't fight me," or "Don't fight it," it's because something's going on that is counterintuitive or not in line with expectations.

I recall another "don't fight me" incident. I was with my son Ryan in the emergency room of Mission Hospital, watching his face redden by the second. He was pinned by heavy Velcro straps to a wooden backboard. Blood trickled from his nose where a nasogastric tube dripped black charcoal down his throat to soak up the medicine in his stomach that he'd swallowed because it "looked like candy." Worst of all, he had a hurt and accusatory look on his face that pleaded, "Aren't you gonna do something?" Our eyes met, and I told him, "Dad's here, son, and it's going to be okay," so that he could stop fighting the terrible process intended to help him. Ryan had to trust me, and my message was, "Don't fight it."

Amazingly, as we locked eyes and he began releasing himself to my calming presence and instruction, his breathing slowed, the redness in his face returned to his normal color, and he made his peace with the most terrifying experience thus far in his short life. Ryan relaxed.

Or imagine the scene as a nurse tries to stick a syringe with vaccine into a panicked child's arm or a mom tries to extract a splinter shoved deep under the skin of her daughter's finger. Any way you experience it, "Don't fight me" is synonymous with the discomfort and suffering that are *necessary* for other positive things to happen. It's an emotional stretch, especially if you are the one getting poked, plucked, or stuck for a "higher purpose." And when love doesn't listen to the cry to make it stop or make it go away, but instead does the painful thing because that's the most loving thing, the reality is disillusioning.

Up in that glider cockpit, God delivered such a message to me. Gary didn't know how I was struggling to get my arms around certain events of my life, my insecurities over the future, and some circumstances engulfing me for the first time. He was just doing his job of helping me fly a glider, but God figured that I would be motivated in such a place to hear a message I desperately needed.

> *When love doesn't listen to the cry to make it stop or make it go away, but instead does the painful thing because that's the most loving thing, the reality is disillusioning.*

Here's the kicker, though: I learned from one of the workers at the airfield that Gary doesn't usually let the uninitiated take the stick on a first flight. But since I was writing a book titled *Soar*, he took a risk, and God seized the opportunity. He's very clever, and His sense of humor knows no bounds!

My spiritual condition that day was reminiscent of an aircraft that is not "trimmed" out. That's pilot lingo for an airplane not adjusted and aligned to match the wind conditions on the nose during flight. An untrimmed aircraft is unwieldy and unstable, thus tough to fly. It will struggle to stay airborne because its rudder, ailerons, and elevator are *fighting the conditions* versus being adjusted to fly *in those conditions*. Sadly, that was my personal condition—unstable and unwieldy under some forceful and unpredictable headwinds in my life.

What exactly was God's Spirit getting at with His "Don't fight Me" message?

Don't fight My purposes in your circumstances.

Don't fight the growth I want to bring about in you.

Don't fight My providence in your life.

Don't fight My authority to mess with your expectations of how you feel your life should be.

Don't fight My voice that is asking you to go against your feelings to be God's Man in this season.

Don't fight Me when I ask you to surrender to this process.

Don't fight the new man I am making *in the midst* of uncomfortable circumstances.

I probably felt like Ryan did when, against his will, he lay strapped on that emergency room backboard, looking into his dad's eyes, fighting to reconcile the panic and pain of the unknown with the strong presence and promise of his father. My son had powerfully conflicting emotions flying head-on into an equally powerful force in his life: me. The more he looked at me, the more peace and resolve he found to endure the process that would save his life from toxic poisoning. The more he listened, the more calm he became.

Ryan stopped fighting. He soared in the midst of disorientation and emotional challenge and came out the other side healed.

Invitation to Elevation

In the day we live, where all of God's Men are challenged economically, culturally, relationally, emotionally, and spiritually, what might the Holy Spirit be saying to you and me?

- You can rise above and face the challenges before you because I have custody over you and your circumstances.
- All undesired, unplanned, and unexpected conditions you find yourself in today are to show the world how My people can rise above all because I AM above all.
- You were created to soar in the midst of, not in the absence of, tribulation and trial.
- You may be weary and confused, but I am strong, confident, and crystal clear about My goals.
- My kingdom will advance most powerfully in you and through you because of your difficulties and challenges, not in spite of them. That is My will.
- So don't fight me! Instead, discover me in the midst of trouble…and soar.

When the Holy Spirit says "Don't fight Me" to God's Man, it is an invitation to elevation. He is saying, "Why act like a common pigeon when I designed you to fly like an eagle?" Remember the words of the prophet Isaiah:

> Do you not know?
> > Have you not heard?
> The LORD is the everlasting God,
> > the Creator of the ends of the earth.
> He will not grow weary,
> > and his understanding no one can fathom.
> He gives strength to the weary
> > and increases the power of the weak.
> Even youths grow tired and weary,
> > and young men stumble and fall;

but those who hope in the LORD
    will renew their strength.
They will soar on wings like eagles;
    they will run and not grow weary,
    they will walk and not be faint. (Isaiah 40:28–31)

This promise was directed at God's people as they faced dynamic and challenging times. In a similar way, in the midst of disillusioning and uncertain times, all men need to make adjustments. The main adjustment is to determine how to connect what's happening to them personally to the larger life context so they can meaningfully live in the midst of their challenges. They need to be "trimmed out," adjusted, and realigned to fly into some serious wind. If a man doesn't do this, he's going to succumb to the gravities of life on earth, lose altitude, and fall out of the sky.

Through His man Isaiah, God said to His people then and to God's Men today:

You can choose to soar or crash in the midst.

Remember who I am.

Dial Me in and listen to me.

Wait upon My word to you and receive it.

Let Me "trim you out" so that you can fly high in these conditions.

Make the adjustments I tell you to make.

I will stabilize, strengthen, and steady you so you can rise above even the most severe winds.

Not many books invite you to welcome and fly directly into the storms of life. Yet you are holding a book that does.

Just like my friend Paul's invitation to take a glider ride was too tempting to pass up, this book is an invitation to experience a different and thrilling dimension of the spiritual life through the power of the Holy Spirit. It may not be what you were looking for, but it just might be what God intended from the moment He created you.

Eagle or Pigeon?

My buddy Dan loves eagles. And while he loves to see them up close in nature, he hates seeing eagles in a cage. His thinking goes like this: a "sitting eagle" is an oxymoron. Imagine being created to soar but being grounded for perpetuity in a zoo. Think about it for a second. This is a bird designed by God to drift, wings spread, effortlessly over mountains, climbing thermals, and covering many miles with ease. As far as birds go, eagles are as strong as they come. They can ascend to altitudes of ten thousand feet or more. They rarely have to flap their wings when migrating to feeding areas, and yet they can hit speeds up to seventy-five miles an hour when descending to nest or munch on a rabbit.

Dan told me about once visiting an eagle cage in a zoo. While comparatively large and expansive to the other holding areas, the cage was totally enclosed with thick black netting and a fence. Curious, Dan asked the handler, "What would happen if the netting and cage were gone?"

> The only way to live such a life of transcendence while on earth is to make a transition in the way you look at life and experience the Holy Spirit's work in and through you. Miss that, and you miss the transcendent life.

"He'd stay right there on the branch," the handler replied. Apparently this eagle was past the point of no return. He had imprinted (or attached) to his environment in captivity and fully recalibrated its natural instinct, desire, and design to soar. This was an eagle acting like a common pigeon. This magnificent creature would never experience the full promise, potential, or power of his design. He would rather perch than fly.

My purpose in this book is to remind every God's Man that he is an eagle, not a pigeon. The problem is that we have millions of men who are eagles that have imprinted, practically and spiritually, like they are pigeons. They are majestic, highly created servants of God who are acting out of character, contrary to their design, wings tucked, and imprisoned by their own bad thinking about themselves and their God. They are swallowing the lies of their feelings, flesh, and fantasies about who they really are and what they are really supposed to be experiencing. The result:

- Low-level living
- Low-level hope
- Low-level discipline
- Low-level spiritual growth
- Low-level risk
- Low-level witness to the world
- Low-level Christianity

This is all wrong. We are able to rise above and live differently in the midst of the earth because we are connected to the most high God. Every person ever born is created to live in this realm, connected to the eternal, transcendent God. That person can, because of this connection, transcend, rise above, and live figuratively like an eagle among pigeons. Why? He is intimately connected to the winds and workings of the Holy Spirit. The only way to live such a life of transcendence while on earth is to make a transition in the way you look at life and experience the Holy Spirit's work in and through you. Miss that, and you miss the transcendent life.

Amid the winds of change and challenge, God's Man must activate, partner, and grow with the Holy Spirit—God's active power on earth. Practically, we do this by embracing the four key SOAR principles that will be outlined throughout this book:

Say yes to the Holy Spirit now…make a switch.

Open new doors to the Holy Spirit…make way.

Actively pursue the Holy Spirit…make strong.

Release the power of the Holy Spirit…make a powerful impact.

Got that? Make a switch. Make way. Make strong. Make a powerful impact. These are the ways in which God's Man trims out his faith to ride the winds of change and challenge. Each action is spelled out clearly in the flight operations manual (Bible) so you can ascend to the exact altitudes of faith and growth as God's Man in the midst of earth. No need to fear these heights.

Equally plain in the Scripture is the fact that the Spirit-formed life will always be challenged by the storms, natural gravities, and injustices of life. That means, as spelled out in the other books in this series (*Risk, Dream,* and *Fight*), these principles and accompanying disciplines are not an event but a way of life for God's Man.

Final Orientation

God comes to man most powerfully in the midst of his darkest hours and biggest challenges, calling him to trim out his faith and fly into the wind. Versus what? Fragmenting or panicking in the midst of trials, choosing to speak and act "pigeon," and ending up planted comfortably on a ten-foot perch in a cage (looking goofy). The difference between flapping hard to stay aloft in the air versus soaring in a different dimension is knowing how your faith is designed to respond in the midst of some heavy winds.

> ### soar fact
> *Just as gravity is necessary to experience lift, so change and challenge are necessary for God's Man to soar spiritually and experience growth through the Holy Spirit.*

Writing this book has compelled me to take a long, hard look in the mirror and ask, "Am I living like an eagle or a pigeon? I want this book to help you ask the same question and make you reflect seriously on how you are going to approach your spiritual journey with God.

You will experience God confronting and then encouraging. Most likely, He will give you a laboratory to test and prove what you are learning in real time. He will throw some delay and difficulty into the mix if you are not already there. He's a great dad, and good dads know how to shape boys into men. So as we enter the arena of Holy

Spirit growth, the encouragement from the Scripture and me is that squirming is expected, but staying in the process makes a man.

> Endure hardship as discipline; God is treating you as sons. For what son is not disciplined by his father? If you are not disciplined (and everyone undergoes discipline), then you are illegitimate children and not true sons. Moreover, we have all had human fathers who disciplined us and we respected them for it. How much more should we submit to the Father of our spirits and live! (Hebrews 12:7–9)

So how about you? Are you ready to get off that perch and spread those wings? Your Father, through His Spirit, wants to say to you, "Could I have a word with you, son?"

It is time to accept the power and soar higher. Don't fight Him.

make way

There is nothing like the power of the Holy Spirit. Only let it come,
and indeed, everything can be accomplished.

—CHARLES SPURGEON

This was to be a strange conversation.

Even though Jesus knew He might get the confused look, He had to download a
complex file of spiritual information with His guys. In computer-speak, you could
say He might nearly crash their hard drives. Jesus communicated as clearly as He
could, but that didn't prevent Him from sounding strange.

Imagine being told by someone very close to you: "Okay, so here's the deal. You
won't be seeing Me anymore. But remember, the fact of the matter is that I am
going, but really, I am not going anywhere. I will be with you even though I am
physically not going to be with you. I will be in you in the form of a Holy Spirit."

Huh? Today, people who say such things are likely to be checked into the nearest
psychiatric facility and given insane amounts of psychotropic medication.

Fortunately for Jesus, He had accrued three years of relational capital that bought
Him a supersized portion of that precious commodity entrusted to all great visionary
leaders: the benefit of the doubt. Jesus knew His message would confuse His men,

but He went for it anyway. He had to, because while what He was telling them sounded strange, it was an inevitable reality His followers would soon have to embrace and experience. Here's the recorded conversation:

> And I will ask the Father, and he will give you another Counselor to be with you forever—the Spirit of truth. The world cannot accept him, because it neither sees him nor knows him. But you know him, for he lives with you and will be in you. I will not leave you as orphans; I will come to you. (John 14:16–18)

When I read in the New Testament about how the disciples were not "getting it" as Jesus spoke of leaving them and sending the Holy Spirit to lead them in His absence, I feel their pain. When the Son of God is talking, no man wants to not get it. But there was simply no context for them to filter such an abstract reality and concept. The result? Scripture says He lost them (for the moment)!

Similarly, millions of believers today struggle to put the intellectual, spiritual, relational, and functional pieces together when it comes to the Holy Spirit. A living Spirit leading them from within is still abstract, misunderstood, misapplied, or not applied at all. It is comforting but also challenging to know that, as history affirms, the disciples' confusion was transformed into experiential clarity and power. Having this knowledge of the future is why Jesus could say near the end of His final huddle with the disciples, "It is for your good that I am going away" (John 16:7). But at the time, and without the same foresight, that was a big stretch for the disciples.

Of course, now, with a couple thousand years of hindsight, what Jesus said makes perfect sense. We know now that the disciples, in their relationship to the Holy Spirit, went from dysfunctional to very dynamic and functional. That is my goal too, and it should be yours as well. It doesn't matter whether you are a new believer or a pastor like me. The age of leadership by the Spirit is the one that you and I are supposed to be experiencing personally right now. So the next

soar fact

"It is for your good that I am going away" means Jesus believed He would do more good in men spiritually than being with men physically.

question all believers must ask themselves is, How's that process of following the Holy Spirit going?

All followers of Christ must come to this particular crossroad: the reality of how relationship with God is set up to work and their responsibility to experience and express it as He intends. Anything less is arrogant or ignorant. More specifically, it accepts the fact that the completion of God's purposes in and through you rests on the quality of your relationship and connection to the Holy Spirit.

And like those first twelve God's Men, we must stretch our faith and embrace the kingdom program as it is, not as we would like it. It is better for us, too, that Jesus is gone and the Holy Spirit is here in His place to lead us. It is better for us that we believe without physically seeing Jesus in order to inherit a richer blessing. It is better for us to live a transcendent, Spirit-filled life of faith in Christ amid the issues of earth. It is better for the people of this world to have Christ accessible and available through the Holy Spirit. It is better for salvation and transformation worldwide that the Holy Spirit is "large and in charge" until Jesus physically returns and His kingdom comes.

Here's the kicker. From God's perspective, it doesn't matter if you fully grasp all of this truth, but He certainly wants you to.

Fortunately, for our journey, we have a bit more context and a few more handles than the disciples did—as well as a few less excuses. And while we still need to learn through application and practice, our four SOAR principles are going to provide us with some serious lift.

SOAR Principle 1: Say Yes to the Holy Spirit

God's Man says "yes" to God's gift.

It doesn't matter how you arrive at that decision. You can arrive there logically, as in "He's God, I'm not; He says it, and that settles it." Or you can arrive there out of the pain your own self-sufficiency has caused you, as in "I don't want to make that mistake again or be that person anymore." For God, intelligent or emotional responses are both secondary to informed responses. Once informed, as God's Men we are responsible to act on the truth as we know it. So let's get informed!

> Therefore do not be foolish, but understand what the Lord's will is. Do not get drunk on wine, which leads to debauchery. Instead, be filled with the Spirit. Speak to one another with psalms, hymns and spiritual songs. Sing and make music in your heart to the Lord, always giving thanks to God the Father for everything, in the name of our Lord Jesus Christ. (Ephesians 5:17–20)

When we say yes to the Holy Spirit, it is important to remember that the decision—by default—is a no as well. Anytime we say yes to God, we are saying no to impulse, culture, man pleasing, and the devil. It's also a no to self-management. And that's the main issue when it comes to our relationship with the Holy Spirit and the ability to meet the changes and challenges we face. In the midst

soar fact
God's will is for all believers to say yes to the Holy Spirit's control of their life. Only a fool says no.

of life we have to ask: "Who's the boss—*really?*" "Who's calling the shots—*really?*" "Who is in control—*really?*"

Remember my flight instructor's words to me in the cockpit of the glider? "Don't fight me."

That is what the Holy Spirit is saying to you right now in some area of your life. The kingdom of God is intended to explode in and through you, but you need to make the transfer of control official. "What transfer?" you ask. The one where we say no to pride and self-sufficiency and say yes to humble and healthy dependency upon the Holy Spirit. Practically, that means you should ask yourself:

Have I said yes to the Holy Spirit's control and asked Him to fill me?

Have I been acting under my own control or His control?

Have I been self-sufficient or humbly dependent on Him?

Have I been fighting God's voice in my life?

Have I been listening to other voices?

It may come as good news to you that all believers must ask themselves these questions on a regular, often daily basis! And if we get derailed, we can get back on track by simply transitioning control to the Holy Spirit. Because God asks this of us, we do it willingly, obediently, and expectantly, because we know He rewards faith.

So now I encourage you to stop, ask the questions, pause for reflection, and issue your:

Declaration of Surrender

> Holy Spirit, I know I need You. I know that I am tempted to be in control of my life, and when I am, I miss out on Your work in me and through me. I am sorry for taking over when I shouldn't. Thank You for Your continuous presence and willingness to direct my life. I ask, Holy Spirit, that You take control of my life right now and fill me. Lead me, guide me, speak to me, open my eyes to God's plan, and help me choose it today. Thank You for taking control and filling me. I ask in Jesus's name. Amen.

SOAR Principle 2: Open Doors

Ever had a door shut on you?

At the ripe old age of ten, I accidentally killed my older sister's parakeet. Now imagine my frantic, manic, and out-of-control older sister chasing yours truly throughout the house, threatening to rearrange my face while spewing unflattering sibling epithets meant to do one thing: make me wish I had never swatted that parakeet off her shoulder. All of this while running at a breakneck pace inside the house.

And did I mention she's gaining on me?

The chase is on, and I can't run outside (she'll lock me out). Can't run into the garage (she'll corner me). Can't run to my room (no lock on the door). Where can the little parakeet killer find refuge?

The bathroom!

If I can just get to the hall with enough room to slam the door shut and turn the lock... GO! Run like the wind! Get there! Almost there...I...am...in! Slam the door! Quick! Twist the lock! ...*WA-BAM!* (The delicious sound of my sister crashing into the door.) HUGE sigh of relief... Demonic voice uttering, "You better open that door, Kenny!" Phew! One of us is very safe. The other is *very* frustrated!

Sadly, this little chase scene resembles what many followers of Jesus do to the Holy Spirit, who—in dramatic contrast to my sister—wants to help them. Instead of opening doors and inviting Him into their different arenas of life, they are slamming the door shut to His influence, and in the process, they are closing the door on His leading, healing, and transforming power.

They might have shame over stuff they have done, guilt over people they have hurt, bitterness over being hurt by others, frustration over their inability to change, or anger toward God because He messed with their expectations of the life they wanted to lead. Like Kenny Boy, they have run to a false safety zone knowing they'll have to come out someday. Stubbornly they are choosing not to let a friend come into their problem areas with His grace to heal and His truth to transform. They have closed the door on the Holy Spirit's work.

There's a term for that: *compartmentalized.* In my book *Fight* I called it a "dark corner." In God's people, it expresses itself in selective obedience, pick-and-choose Christianity, or a "what happens in private, stays private"–type of self-delusion.

When I became a follower of Jesus, I read Revelation 3:20 and got it. Jesus said, "Here I am! I stand at the door and knock. If anyone hears my voice and opens the door, I will come in and eat with him, and he with me."

That's an awesome word picture of us standing inside our home and hearing a knock. Curious, we go to the door and ask the expected question: "Who is it?"

"It's Me, Jesus. Can I come in?"

Then we willingly and voluntarily open the door and connect. That's a shared moment all believers have with Jesus. There is a moment of welcome, a time of belief, acceptance, and integration of Christ into our life.

For years I related that verse only to my conversion until I realized that the knocking didn't end at salvation and neither did the opening of doors. That first knock and invitation into the life was just the first big door, which was soon followed by hundreds of more knocks, as Jesus, with my permission through the Holy Spirit, went on a tour of the other rooms of my life:

- Room of secrets
- Room of private habits
- Room of insecurities
- Room of character
- Room of beliefs
- Room of relationships
- Room of marriage
- Room of thought life
- Room of unhealthy appetites
- Room of the past

Jesus knocked for salvation, and I said, "Yes, c'mon in!" The Spirit took up residence in me, kept knocking, and began the renovation and transformation projects in all my other rooms!

SOAR Principle 3: Actively Pursue

It's easy to get into relationships. It's another thing to make them work.

All of us have been confronted by this reality. Men are especially guilty of treating a relationship as something to be conquered and then set aside in order to conquer the next goal. For example, in wooing a wife, we love the pursuit and the winning of the prize. But then we often struggle with the proper maintenance of the marriage. The very things we need, want, and measure relationships by are also the very things we find hard to deliver: personal time, touch, and talk.

So many times I have thought I was doing something meaningful for Chrissy only to discover that it was more meaningful to me than it was to her! I was with her, and I thought she was *with me,* but we actually were miles apart. My idea of a strong relationship was my protection and provision, while her idea of a strong relationship was time and talk. Mars and Venus weren't connecting deeply, and in the process, we disconnected and started self-destructing.

Fortunately, the light went on just in time. Sometimes we forget that the Holy Spirit is a Person with desires, intellect, and emotions, who will require understanding for intimacy.

Persons require interaction. God is self-described in the Bible as Persons (Father, Son, and Holy Spirit) who are intimately interacting. The three actively pursue, help, support, interact, and express their individuality in unity. We see them all in play at the baptism of Jesus: the creative mind of the Father, the agent of expression getting dunked, and the active power of the Holy Spirit.

> **soar fact**
> *Deep relationship is synonymous with meaningful interaction.*

After his baptism, as Jesus came up out of the water, the heavens were opened and he saw the Spirit of God descending like a dove and settling on him. And a voice from heaven said, "This is my dearly loved Son, who brings me great joy." (Matthew 3:16–17, NLT)

We see this intimate partnership in the New Testament, made visible in the life of Jesus. He is always making the effort to connect and partner with the members of the Godhead (Father and Spirit). We see Him saying yes to the Holy Spirit's leadership into the wilderness in Luke 4. We see Him constantly stealing away to dialogue with and find comfort in His Abba Father. They all do life together. And while they are perfectly one—content and sufficiently connected in themselves—they *want and desire a strong relationship with us:*

> And I will ask the Father, and he will give you another Counselor to be with you forever—the Spirit of truth. The world cannot accept him, because it neither sees him nor knows him. But you know him, for he lives with you and will be in you. I will not leave you as orphans; I will come to you. (John 14:16–18)

That's what you call teamwork for a good cause. Each person of the Trinity in agreement, moving as one, target selected, and on mission to reach into your life with their unique qualities and personality as a united presence.

The Holy Spirit wants a strong relationship with you. Get that. Versus what? Versus a weak, meaningless, casual, intellectual, unthoughtful association. A relationship with the Holy Spirit is only made strong through an aggressive and intentional pursuit of that relationship by the believer.

Men know those two words (*aggressive* and *intentional*) when it comes to securing a relationship or winning a member of the opposite sex. The things we do (or did) for love!

- We listened.
- We talked late into the night.
- We created "moments."

- We sacrificed other commitments.
- We went to great lengths to connect.
- We were driven to understand.

You get the picture. And this intensity in relationship is what the Holy Spirit wants in connecting with you. Aggressively and intentionally pursuing a strong relationship with Him will involve

- meditation in His inspired Word (listening).
- interaction with Him through prayer (conversing).
- affirmation of His person and purpose in your life (validating).
- cooperation with Him in the midst of temptation (partnering).

That's a real relationship with a real person!

You might be thinking, Hey, Kenny, I do all those disciplines already! How does this relationship with the Holy Spirit differ—if at all—from my relationship with God the Father and Jesus?

My answer and challenge is threefold. First, recognize that without the Holy Spirit no conscious contact or relationship with God is possible. He is the chip, so to speak, that makes it possible for you to run all the software applications of spiritual life. He illuminates "all things God" for man.

Second, address, respond, and interact with the Holy Spirit personally and equally as you would with Jesus Christ or God the Father. If I were the Holy Spirit, I might feel like chopped liver by the way believers leave Him strangely absent in their prayers and practice of the faith. After I had taught a lesson on the Holy Spirit, a man asked me, "Is it okay if I pray directly to the Holy Spirit?" I replied, "Of course!"

Third, release yourself personally to the Holy Spirit's specific works of God in your life, just as Scripture highlights and commands.

We will practice all three of these in every chapter to cultivate your interactions with the Holy Spirit.

SOAR Principle 4: Release the Power

I am attracted to powerful things.

The short list includes tornadoes, jet fighters, big guns, explosives, linebackers (in a "bromantic" way), meteors, rhinos, aircraft carriers, mixed martial arts fighters, monster slam dunks, hurricanes, earthquakes, knockouts, hip-hop dancing, the big waves at Maverick's, William Wallace, rodeo bulls, M1 Abrams main battle tanks, mama grizzly bears, class-five rapids, silverback gorillas, and the Holy Spirit.

Now, maybe you are wondering: Did Luck just slide the Holy Spirit onto that list?

Yes, I did.

The Holy Spirit made it onto that list because He does things that make my jaw extend, my lungs take in crazy amounts of air, my mouth pucker, my voice shout, and my head shake in mind-bending disbelief at—you guessed it—the POW-UH, baby! I see the things He does to people. I see the answers to prayer He brings. I see relationships He heals. And I have seen and experienced the powerful changes His presence has produced in my own family, life, and relationships.

No powerful force can compare to the fierce and awesome power of the Holy Spirit's filling a man, changing that man forever, and exploding God's love back out of that man into the world to advance the kingdom of God. That is what Jesus said would happen to every believer who makes strong his relationship to the Holy Spirit:

> But you will receive power when the Holy Spirit comes on you; and you will be my witnesses in Jerusalem, and in all Judea and Samaria, and to the ends of the earth. (Acts 1:8)

One of the highest privileges of pastoring men worldwide is that I have seen Jesus's words concerning the explosive work of the Holy Spirit's effect on men come true on a weekly basis. As I write these words, my mind drifts immediately to a man named Erik.

I met Erik at the request of friends who had run into him at our church's annual men's conference. My friends said Erik wanted to meet me, so we took a small table in the corner of a crowded coffeehouse. Erik wasted no time in explaining his encounter with the Holy Spirit during the meeting we had just left a few hours earlier. I asked him point-blank, "When did you cross the line and begin to follow Jesus Christ?"

"Tonight at the service," Erik responded. From there he recounted the long, painful, and self-destructive journey to this moment and how he had been filled with power at the meeting in a way he had never experienced before.

As a competitive triathlete, he was used to forging ahead in isolation and competing within and against himself. But even for the strongest of mind and body, there is always the challenge of relationships that no amount of training or achievement can heal or make work without character. This, it appeared, was in short supply in Erik's life, and he was, as he put it, bankrupt when it came to his relationships and as a new dad.

Enter the Holy Spirit's invading presence into this man's life with a decision to surrender his life to Christ! Since then, not only does Erik not run from his relational challenges, but he engages them with a new eye toward God's will over his will and impulses. Through a process of studying the Bible, asking to be filled with the Holy Spirit, and progressively opening doors to God's presence and lordship, Erik has secured for the first time in his life something that had eluded him for twenty years: self-control. This may seem like a small matter, but for Erik it was both a demon and a Goliath that he could not slay on his own.

Now Erik isn't thirty-five going on thirteen anymore, running away from responsibility and making self-destructive choices to make himself feel better by medicating pain. He has traded in those ways of being for God's purposes and the power of the Holy Spirit.

But the Holy Spirit's work in Erik also blasted *out* of him with equal power, as Erik sought to reach men for Christ through his passion for the triathlon. The same month Erik made a commitment to follow Christ, he began thinking of ways he could reach other men for Christ and ways to encourage both men and women to follow Him more passionately. The result was that he founded Multisport Ministries (MSM). What started as a small group of men meeting at races to encourage each other in their faith mushroomed into a fellowship and outreach more than seven hundred strong in its second year. This group, which includes some of the world's top triathletes, is making its presence felt and God's promises known in the water, on the bike, and on the pavement.

With their bright yellow and black jerseys dotting the USA Triathlon Tour, MSM has over twenty chapters encouraging athletes, building a witness for Christ, and winning souls. Through the power and promise of the Holy Spirit, one transformed man is transforming many lives, just as Jesus predicted.

You, I, and every believer brave enough to go deeper with God must make the transition toward a powerful and transcendent relationship with the Holy Spirit. *That* is the plan.

A Look from Up Top

Let's pause for a second.

I want you to imagine taking an elevator to the top of a skyscraper. When you step outside, you take in the panorama and point out places you want to go. That's what I want to do before we go on. We need to take a look at where we are, where we are headed, and what our goals are for the rest of the journey before we take the ride back down and head out.

This first section of *Soar* will continue to explore the **transition** in your thinking about the Holy Spirit in an intentional and biblical effort to reframe Him. The goal: to go from dysfunctional or even functional over to personally informed and more meaningful. This will mean drilling deep into

- His presence and purpose in your life right now.
- your relationship and responsibilities to Him right now.
- the application and appropriation of the Holy Spirit right now.
- how to recognize and respond to the Holy Spirit's voice.

You will see and sense Him like never before.

The second section will focus on the work the Holy Spirit seeks to accomplish in you, or the **transformation** of character that allows a Spirit-formed person to rise above the gravity of change and challenge. You will become a new person.

The third section will address the work the Holy Spirit seeks to accomplish through you: the powerful **transactions** God has designed for this relationship to bring about for His kingdom and for His church. You will unleash God's power and, in the process, leave an eternal footprint as an ambassador for the gospel of Jesus.

My prayer is that by the time you reach the end of this book, you will be so connected to the Holy Spirit that you will be catching His drift in the most powerful and purposeful ways, soaring steadily and strongly in the midst of your life to make a major impact. That is, that you show yourself to be Christ's disciple.

double-check

It is worse still to be ignorant of your own ignorance.

—JEROME (AD 347–420)

It was time.

My family had been waiting all Christmas morning to get to this moment. And I was the object of a powerful conspiracy inspired by my wife. The mission: lull me into a vulnerable state of mind, make it appear as if Christmas was over, and then ambush me with a gift I would never expect. Playing disinterested, playing it cool, and expertly concealing their excitement, my family hooked me into their benevolent deception like a largemouth bass.

Innocently, Chrissy said, "So is that it? Are we done with presents?"

I added energy to their plot by saying, "I think that just about does it."

Then Chrissy did what everyone in our family would expect her to do: double-check. "Ryan, will you look under the tree for me and make sure we have everything?"

"Yup… Hey, there's one more. Has Dad's name on it," said Ryan as he stretched his hand under the tree to their hiding spot, secured the little box, and proceeded to hand it to Chrissy.

"Oh, that. Let me see it. I almost forgot to wrap this. Just a little something. Open it up, Kenny."

From all appearances, everyone acted like this was an afterthought, unimportant, and as underwhelming as Chrissy made it seem. Chalk it up to great acting. Inside my family, however, there was a growing tsunami of excitement betraying this calm ocean of disinterestedness. A monumental surprise was about to hit the sleepy shores of a country known as "Dadzaria." Can't you feel it? Imagine a lone man blissfully playing on the shore while a surging wall of water is about to swallow him. That was me.

Ignorance is to surprise what oxygen is to life: essential.

It was a four-by-six-inch box, and I was thinking it truly was a "little" something. If it were something big, Chrissy would have been obligated to consult with me, due to the money factor. That was the rule, I thought, and that was why the others were about to wet themselves. So with the ruse now accelerating to mach speed, I casually and only semicuriously started pulling the wrapping off the box.

Rip. Is that an Apple logo? Can't be.

A second rip. That is an Apple logo!

A third rip. It can't be an iPhone?

Final rip. *KUH-BOOM!* It *was* an iPhone!

Like runaway trains on the same tracks, two completely different sets of expectations and emotions now collided. I literally crumpled. My family watched me slump over, collapse my face into my hands, and mutter "No way!" over and over again.

On the other side of the room came an explosion of laughter. This is the physics of a good surprise. Head buried still, I could hear Chrissy saying something to me about points she discovered from a credit card rewards program that made the iPhone gift possible.

I still couldn't talk, and now the "no cash out" factor sweetened the moment even more.

"No way! No way!"

My family had achieved Christmas shell shock: man holding small box, mouth open, staring at a half-wrapped present, plus a goofy facial expression that said happy, surprised, and grateful all at once.

I was a kid again.

Just a Little Something

What a moment.

There was so much excitement on the part of my family for me to unwrap, discover, and be energized by their gift. Funny thing was, at the same exact moment I was barely motivated, indifferent, and a bit apathetic. It was a case of "raring to go" meets dispassionate and blasé in a head-on collision. What a combination!

The result: pleasantly surprised.

A thoughtful gift will do that. A creative gift will do that. A well-timed gift will do that. A high-quality gift will do that. Unexpected gifts will really do that.

As we explore how the person and power of the Holy Spirit move within and upon your life, you are coming to the discussion from one of three places: (a) you are taking an exploratory look into the Holy Spirit, (b) you're double-checking (maybe triple-checking) to see if there's more under the tree for you, or (c) you fit both the *a* and *b* categories. Regardless of where you are coming from, I want you to know one thing: there is a little something for you coming.

How do I know? I will let the apostle Peter do the explaining:

Peter replied, "Repent and be baptized, every one of you, in the name of Jesus Christ for the forgiveness of your sins. *And you will receive the gift of the Holy Spirit.*" (Acts 2:38)

Why say it like that? Why dangle that at the end? It's like Peter is pitching one of those deals you might see in the makeup section of Macy's or Bloomingdale's. It is the infamous "gift with purchase." Ladies can't resist this. The deal is very attractive: lay down the cash for one thing, and we will throw in something very special with your purchase (a beach bag, a bottle of perfume, an umbrella, or a special basket of assorted lotions). Make no mistake, gifts with purchase (GWP for short) hook big numbers of previously uninterested fish in the retail game. The idea of getting something special added on to a purchase of something I already want makes me want to purchase that something even more.

How does this relate to the Holy Spirit?

God accepts only one currency for salvation: faith. Repentance and baptism were and still are authentic expressions of faith in the person and work of Christ. The result: salvation and forgiveness of sins. Many of those listening to Peter must have been thinking, *Sounds good to me,* and they wanted in right

> *God accepts only one currency for salvation: faith.*

there. But Peter continued forcefully: "And that's not all. With that one, sincere expression of faith, in addition to forgiveness of sins, God wants to give you a second gift as well. You will receive…(drumroll, please) the gift of the Holy Spirit!"

Now we have just gone from bunches of people to bushels of new believers. Check it out: "Those who accepted his message were baptized, and about three thousand were added to their number that day" (Acts 2:41).

Under God's direction, Peter delivered what the French call the *pièce de résistance,* which refers to the best part or the best feature about something or some experience. I mean, it was good already, right? Who doesn't want forgiveness of sin and permanent peace with God? But just as a good number probably started making their way forward, Peter dropped the bomb—the *pièce de résistance* of God's salvation and transformation plan called the gift of the Holy Spirit. Just the idea of a mysterious gift tripled the anticipation level of those listening.

Peter was soaring full of the Spirit, the crowd was flying high in anticipation of the Spirit, and all present were expectant of a move of the Spirit. One little sentence afforded everyone listening a titanic opportunity: God Himself offering to every person a gift that could be received, unwrapped, and embraced right now.

The Holy Spirit is described in the Bible as a gift. God knew what He wanted to say at that exciting moment in history, and He chose Peter's words very carefully for him. God's *pièce de résistance* for believers then and for all time would be the indwelling gift of the Holy Spirit Himself, received upon belief in Christ. As a gift, the Holy Spirit would

soar fact
Gifts are synonymous with anticipation and excitement. Gifts create hope and contain the mysterious "new." That is the nature of a gift.

- be the absolute best part of our experience with God.
- make faith in Christ anything but routine.
- provide a personalized, unique spiritual experience.
- load up our faith with new expectancy.
- draw us into deeper and more special connection with God.
- create an eagerness for spiritual matters.
- bring a different dimension of living in the midst of our earthly existence.
- be unending in His unfolding of change in the life of the believer.

This last quality is what made Peter's statement so powerful and what distinguishes the Holy Spirit's work from the other works of God that are transacted upon initial faith in Christ. In fact, over thirty irrevocable things happen spiritually to us at the moment of salvation. These spiritual blessings include: being completely forgiven of all sin, eternal life, made a child of God, given access to the Father, reconciled to God, justified before God, placed "in Christ" forever, redeemed, adopted by God, delivered from darkness, and granted heavenly citizenship—just to name a few. It's amazing to think that simultaneously and instantaneously our faith produces such a lavish inheritance through association with Christ.

Then, in the midst of the apostle Peter's bold announcement, there is a hard stop, a period, and a transition takes place. More specifically, Peter goes from describing one of the salvation works wrought by God (forgiveness) to describing the ongoing transformational work that will continue in the believer through the receiving of the gift of the Holy Spirit. This work or gift is not a one-time event; it is a dynamic, continuous, and ongoing *process*. The gift of the Holy Spirit initiates a succession of continuous character changes that bring about Christlikeness in the believer.

If you want to describe your life as a believer in two simple words, they are *salvation* and *transformation*. We are saved once through faith, but we are being transformed continually by the Holy Spirit.

> And we, who with unveiled faces all reflect the Lord's glory, are being transformed into his likeness with ever-increasing glory, which comes from the Lord, *who is the Spirit.* (2 Corinthians 3:18)

I point this out now because you may have thoughts like these during this discussion of the Holy Spirit:

- "I know this already."
- "I have this covered."
- "Tell me something I don't already know."
- "I am a pastor."
- "I don't have time."
- "This is a review."
- "This is too complex."
- "This works for someone else but not for me."

When we display the language of self-sufficiency, pride, or apathy when it comes to our journey with the Holy Spirit, by default we forfeit the transformation He wants to give us. Let me put this gently to you, my brotha: I don't want you to miss out on these! More personally, He *always* has "a little something" tucked away for us that will flow out of His person: His infinite, powerful, and gift-giving nature. With Him it's a nonstop progression of revelation and transformation *if* we are willing to embrace what we're offered.

My iPhone gift worked for me in a way similar to the work of the Holy Spirit. The iPhone ad campaign was simple: "Watch this." And, boy, did I watch that commercial in awe. Very attractive. Some dude touching the screen for a call, for the Web, for e-mail, for stock prices, for just about everything. The feel and function as I watched it was magical and magnetic. As you know, powerful things attract me, including powerful technology. So when my new power toy landed in my lap, it was a process of getting to know exactly what I was holding and how to integrate all that powerful technology into my daily flow.

> *When we display the language of self-sufficiency, pride, or apathy when it comes to our journey with the Holy Spirit, by default we forfeit the transformation He wants to give us.*

At first it was just about using the phone, entering all my contacts, learning the icons, and picking a ringtone—the basics of any phone today. Then came the process of engaging the alarm and stopwatch, the camera, the calculator, the weather function, and the calendar. The next phase was followed by Google maps, driving directions, text messaging, Internet usage, and e-mailing from anywhere in the world. Within months I figured out how to load all of my favorite songs and movies. And now, there is a progressive stream of "apps," some of which serve me every day.

All this excitement is from a guy who, not that long ago, was terrified of technology, unfamiliar with the word *interface,* and feeling left out of a revolution so many others were enjoying. And while it took me a full year to become a fully "orbed" user of my iPhone, this powerful technology has radically altered (in a good way) the way I live and function. How? I am always being offered a new experience through new features of its technology. It even automatically checks for updates so that I can experience its latest capacities and applications every two weeks.

My experience with my iPhone is one of *progressive revelation.*

Now, let's be clear. I know there is a limit I am reaching with my iPhone with respect to its capabilities. However, no such limits exist with the powerful tool given to every believer in the person of the Holy Spirit. In fact, Jesus said that the flow of the Holy Spirit's work in your life would be like a natural spring that bubbles out continuous, life-giving change that would leak out of us and onto others and into the world.

> "If anyone is thirsty, let him come to me and drink. Whoever believes in me, as
> the Scripture has said, streams of living water will flow from within him." By
> this he meant the Spirit, whom those who believed in him were later to receive.
> (John 7:37–39)

Jesus was foreshadowing this coming piece of spiritual technology called the Holy Spirit. He would be a radical producer of spiritual life for believers thirsty for change *without limit.* Like a natural spring that steadily bubbles the pure stuff out of the ground, your journey with the person of the Holy Spirit is one of *progressive knowledge of His person and continuous experiences with His power in your life.* He is intended to be an unbroken and constant revelation of God to believers who have the desire for more of God.

So whether you are acquainting yourself with the capacities of the Holy Spirit for the first time or double-checking under your spiritual tree for some new surprise, every seeker of God is assured of new life through the Spirit, new experiences with the Spirit, and new expressions of the Spirit. *One desire unites us all: a hunger for deeper works of God in our lives.*

> **soar fact**
> *There's more of God for those
> who desire more—courtesy
> of the Holy Spirit.*

The sad fact is that while the Holy Spirit lives in all believers, millions have failed to understand what they actually possess. At some point after salvation they stopped pursuing the relationship, and this powerful force is left dormant, untapped, and grossly underutilized. And just as standing water becomes polluted and toxic without a flow, believers will become stagnant and polluted by other influences without the steady streams of water washing over their life.

Others among us have forgotten to check for any updates when prompted, and they have lived off of old versions of His work far too long. As a consequence, the progressive revelation of the Holy Spirit in our lives has stopped, and we feel left behind as we attempt to live off the spiritual leftovers of past experiences.

It's time for something fresh.

The Fresh Stuff

I am into fresh.

Fresh coffee, because it tastes way better. Fresh bread, because it's way softer. Fresh clothes, because they smell good. Fresh air, because it's crisp and clean. Fresh sheets, because they feel good. Fresh thoughts, because I need and love good ideas. And fresh maple bars from DK Donuts, because they taste so good!

Some of this stuff turns over daily, like the French bread at the local market. In fact, on the package it says, "Baked fresh at 4 p.m. daily." Other things are serviced every few days or weekly. The milk in my fridge has expiration dates that indicate when "fresh" is over and "old" has begun.

The enemy of fresh is *old*.

There is no such thing as "old" Holy Spirit, only new. That's why we can say yes to the Holy Spirit every day, because He is serving up the fresh stuff that you need daily in order to live out God's purposes. In fact, He has an infinite supply of what you need every day for the changes and challenges you face.

What are some fresh items available from the Holy Spirit? I want some!

- **Fresh leadership from Jesus:** "If you love me, you will obey what I command. And I will ask the Father, and he will give you another Counselor to be with you forever—the Spirit of truth. The world cannot accept him, because it neither sees him nor knows him. But you know him, for he lives with you and will be in you. I will not leave you as orphans; I will come to you" (John 14:15–18).

  Just say: "Holy Spirit, I need Your presence and leadership in this season, today, or right now in this moment. In all my conversations and interactions, lead me and control me. Guide me, Holy Spirit."

- **Fresh advice:** "But I tell you the truth: It is for your good that I am going away. Unless I go away, the Counselor will not come to you; but if I go, I will send him to you" (John 16:7).

  Just say: "Holy Spirit, I need Your strong and clear counsel about _____ today. Point me to Your Word and show me Your will in the Scripture. Connect me with another believer, someone who's filled with You and listens to You. Let me sense You talking to me through my conscience, and help me to receive what You say and to follow Your counsel today."

- **Fresh truth:** "But when he, the Spirit of truth, comes, he will guide you into all truth. He will not speak on his own; he will speak only what he hears, and he will tell you what is yet to come. He will bring glory to me by taking from what is mine and making it known to you. All that belongs to the Father is mine. That is why I said the Spirit will take from what is mine and make it known to you" (John 16:13–15).

  Just say: "Holy Spirit, help me to be truthful with myself, God, and others today. Help me to support and connect with what is honest and real in all things. Save me from the lies coming at me and from the lies that come from within me. Help me to remember Your Word today, which is truth. Help me to remember moment by moment that when something is true, it's You. Then help me to accept and act on those things."

- **Fresh forgiveness:** "So now there is no condemnation for those who belong to Christ Jesus. And because you belong to him, the power of the life-giving Spirit has freed you from the power of sin that leads to death" (Romans 8:1–2, NLT).

  Just say: "Holy Spirit, have mercy on me and free me today. I belong to You again right now. I am sorry for grieving You. I have sinned. I receive Your acceptance and forgiveness right now for what I have done, in Jesus's name."

- **Fresh thinking:** "Those who are dominated by the sinful nature think about sinful things, but those who are controlled by the Holy Spirit think about things that please the Spirit. So letting your sinful nature control your mind leads to death. But letting the Spirit control your mind leads to life and peace" (Romans 8:5–6, NLT).

  Just say: "Holy Spirit, I give You my thought life. Control my thoughts and guide them toward what pleases God. Flood my mind today with what is true, honorable, and right. Let me affirm those good things, speak about them, and live them out courageously. Help me to walk away, to turn away, or to run away from anything that takes my thoughts down a wrong path. Lead me to good sources to fill up my mind."

- **Fresh encouragement:** "So you have not received a spirit that makes you fearful slaves. Instead, you received God's Spirit when he adopted you as his own children. Now we call him, 'Abba, Father.' For his Spirit joins with our spirit to affirm that we are God's children" (Romans 8:15–16, NLT).

  Just say: "I am a son of the living God. I am Your son. I love being Your son. Thank You, Father, for Your strong assurance in my life that calms me and reminds me today that I have no reason to fear anyone or anything. You are my Father, I am in your custody, and I trust You. Thank You for loving me completely and totally. Thank You for my sonship. Holy Spirit, help me be a passionate son like Christ."

- **Fresh power to defeat sin:** "So I say, let the Holy Spirit guide your lives. Then you won't be doing what your sinful nature craves" (Galatians 5:16, NLT).

Just say: "Holy Spirit, help me say no to dark desires and say yes to You every step of the day. Help me say yes to You with my feet, my eyes, my words, my patience, and my energy. Guide me away from sin as You guide me to sources of truth and power. Thank You, Holy Spirit, for helping me to defeat the evil within."

The Holy Spirit is not only saying "Don't fight Me," but more invitingly asking us to double-check under the tree one more time. And we can keep coming back for more. From that first Christmas outside of Bethlehem to this moment, the Holy Spirit has been unfolding the gifts of God to man. There is so much excitement on His part for you to unwrap, discover, and be energized by His gifts.

And just as I was on that Christmas morning, at this exact moment you may be barely motivated, indifferent, and a bit apathetic. Well, my brother, just know that raring to go is on the other side of your decision. Your job is simple: receive Him right now into your life in the specific ways God intended. He's the answer to old… stale…lost…defeated…guilty…discouraged. He is the best thing you own.

The Holy Spirit is the *pièce de résistance* of God.

It is time for fresh.

the invisible intangible

His is the power. Ours is the blessing. How we listen will determine it all.

—JACK HAYFORD

Bring it!

That's macho talk for "let's see what you're made of" or "hit me with your best shot." It's calling someone, some process, or something on the carpet in that "put up or shut up" sort of way. Hang around men a little while, and you'll hear one of these phrases or a form of it. Other versions include:

- "Oh, it's on!"
- "Game on!"
- "Let's do this thing!"
- "Let's get it on!"
- "Let's see what you got!"
- "Rock and roll, baby!"
- "You want some of this?"

You get the picture.

Bring it.

On the other side of all this peacocking is the severity of reality. Once the talking stops, the action starts, the truth is told, and some man proves himself. One rises above and the other is humiliated, is vanquished, stops moving, or stops talking (at least for a while). In "manworld," no other activity on the planet exemplifies this type of hype, posturing, and catharsis like contests. Two dudes, mano a mano, "last man standing" types of battle.

For me, two legendary episodes in particular stand out: one from the modern era and one from biblical times. The first is the epic March 8, 1971, boxing match between Muhammad Ali and Joe Frazier known as the Fight of the Century. The other would be best classified as the Fight of the *Centuries,* or David versus Goliath.

These two encounters can be summed up in one word: *antagonism.* And as we'll see in this chapter, this is the best word to describe the real spiritual environment in which God's Men operate.

Muhammad Ali was young, undefeated (31-0), undaunted, and unafraid of anyone, anything, anytime, or anywhere. Goliath had a similar résumé, character, and temperament. These two warriors were brothers from another mother who lived in different ages but possessed a number of things in common. The most obvious include:

- World-class fighters
- Inflated senses of invincibility
- Undefeated records
- Menacing reputations
- Towering physical presences
- Champions of their people or movement
- Masters of psychological warfare
- Always favored to win
- Totally self-absorbed
- Diarrhea of the mouth

This last quality, while graphic, is the most relevant. Go with me! You see, for both of these men, once an opponent was identified, a flood of animosity was discharged. The verbal tirades directed publicly at their opponents were so frequent, so excessive, so demeaning, so visceral, and so foul smelling, you *had* to react.

Nothing was off-limits. The jugular veins they seized included highlighting the social, racial, political, physical, and religious fabric of their opponents, then mocking it and rubbing it generously in their face. Their message was unequivocal: I defy you, I disregard you, and I despise you. In fact, one of Ali's nicknames was the "Louisville Lip," which reflected his penchant for toxic prefight comments and self-congratulation. And while Goliath did not hail from Louisville, he, like Ali, definitely had the lip part perfected.

The butt of their tirades were two other warriors: Joe and David. They, like their foes, were also undefeated. Frazier was 26-0, and David, while still a teenager, had tangled with and killed a lion *and* a bear while shepherding his dad's sheep. "Smokin' Joe" and David could also be classified as brothers from another mother. By studying them, you learn that both were:

- Introverted
- Confident
- Skilled fighters
- God fearers
- Of humble origin
- Not favored to win
- Fearless
- Passionate
- Patriotic
- Compassionate
- Giant killers

For the record, Ali was put on his back, his right jaw shattered by a spectacular left hook by Frazier in the fifteenth round. The hit was so powerful doctors had to wire Ali's mouth shut. That's justice!

Goliath fared much worse, taking a well-placed stone to the forehead, courtesy of David's sling. And all nine feet of this behemoth crashed lifelessly atop Judean soil. His jaw might not have broken, but everyone else's was on the ground. Pure shock and awe. In both cases, the oddsmakers were proven wrong. David and Joe each heard the loud thud of his opponent hitting the ground, not the other way around.

Invisible Intangibles

Young David and Joe Frazier were judged in the court of outward impressions. Neither was fancy. Neither had a commanding presence. Both were outsized, outtalked, and supposedly outgunned. They were grossly underestimated and underappreciated, because both men's greatest asset was not external, visible, or even quantifiable. For starters, neither believed the hype. Neither let in the fear. But in the end, it boiled down to something very subjective: a personal, powerful inner witness in the heart of each man that he could answer the challenge when all those around him remained unconvinced.

For Joe Frazier, his mental preparation for the Fight of the Century was just as intense as his physical preparation. When you watch the fight, there's only one way to describe the shorter, slower, and more methodical Frazier: relentless. Left hook after left hook, body punch after body punch, Frazier worked through Ali's faster punching and better combination work consistently and effectively. Frazier was on a mission, and he

For David, it was not a matter of mental preparation but an activation of his convictions.

would not be denied. His trademark? He just kept coming after you. He was a pit bull with a purpose. Ali's fatal mistake was underestimating Frazier's invisible intangible: his lion's heart.

For David, it was not a matter of mental preparation but an activation of his convictions. He was bringing lunch to his brothers on the frontlines *at the exact moment* when the army was taking up battle positions and shouting the war cry. He was dropping off supplies and greeting for his brothers, and "as he was talking with them, Goliath, the Philistine champion from Gath, stepped out from his lines and shouted out his usual defiance, and David heard it. When the Israelites saw the man, they all ran from him in great fear" (1 Samuel 17:23–24). The beginning of the end for the overconfident champion from Gath is found in three little words: "David heard it."

Goliath's fatal mistake was not accounting for the invisible intangible in the recesses of David's soul: a strong, abiding relationship to his God. The same God Goliath was throwing under the bus. You might ask, How could he have known who he was dealing with? He couldn't have known! Men always ran away from him. That was his experience and thought process. But as the sound waves of Goliath's mocking words slammed into David's ear canal, made their way to his cerebral cortex, and were translated into a clear message for David to process, a tsunami of emotions, energy, and holy inertia was triggered that no one could have predicted. One man in the crowd of the opposing side started moving toward Goliath. And that walk toward battle would quickly turn into a run to battle. David was a complete and total anomaly in every external way. But inwardly, he was being completely consistent and congruent.

The result?

A physical giant and warrior awakened a spiritual giant and would-be warrior, setting up the most outlandish and courageous confrontation in history. Here's how it went down:

> David asked the men standing near him, "What will be done for the man
> who kills this Philistine and removes this disgrace from Israel? Who is this
> uncircumcised Philistine that he should defy the armies of the living God?"
> (1 Samuel 17:26)

Travel with me inside David's brain for a second. The first neuron to fire says: "What! Who is this guy?" The second neuron fires and concludes: "He's going down." And the final mental transaction is: "Who do I tell that I want this dude's head on a platter?"

David's words and actions betray all logic and common sense exactly because they are coming from a deep well of personal conviction, relationship, and loyalty unseen to others. Goliath was disgracing his God—*his* Lord. It's the classic Hollywood setup for a revenge scene: villain mistakenly injures or takes a potshot at someone the hero cares about. *Now, it's personal.* That's why David is diving into the breach while all the professional soldiers are experiencing shrinkage below the belt.

As the story unfolds, it's hard not to notice the response of David's own brothers and their fellow soldiers: they do not have even *one word* of encouragement or affirmation for David. What transpires is comical: *he has to fight for the opportunity to fight!* A man and his invisible intangible are standing alone, and facing the giant.

Goliath is toast.

Running to Battle

Much like David's experience, a New Testament Christian does not exist in an environment of affirmation. He is not supported in his beliefs and practice from a surrounding tribe of faith (which is what the Israelites were supposed to be for David) where everyone in the spiritual vicinity is living according to Scripture. Instead, you and I are designated by the Bible as strangers deployed in a foreign land that is openly hostile to our faith and seeks to tear it to pieces.

> **soar fact**
> *The Holy Spirit is the invisible intangible of God's Man that allows him to confidently face open hostility to his faith and vanquish fear.*

That may not be the way we want it to be, but that is the way it is. The culture *around us,* which is the New Testament man's Goliath, has these characteristics:

- Is hostile to the teachings and principles of Scripture
- Mocks God openly
- Has an identity outside of God
- Possesses values that destroy a relationship with God
- Outsizes, outguns, and outmessages God's Man
- Exists everywhere you turn
- Intimidates faith
- Is used to winning over God's Man

That last one simply does not have to be.

Jesus was up-front about the reality of identity in Him and the reality of cultural hostility:

> As it is, you do not belong to the world, but I have chosen you out of the world. That is why the world hates you.... If they persecuted me, they will persecute you also.... They will treat you this way because of my name, for they do not know the One who sent me. (John 15:19–21)

What Jesus identified as the world is synonymous with the male culture today that does not factor God in on purpose.

Throughout history the term *God's people* is synonymous with open hostility. In fact, reading the Bible can give you a sense that God is easier on His enemies than on His own people. From the time of the Egyptian pharaohs to fascist dictators to communist persecutors to critics who have an open bias and hostility against Christians around the world, God's people have been acquainted with recriminations and suffering. Persecution is the consequence of men with weak ideas who feel their power being threatened. Find men persecuting Christians, and you will find deeply insecure and fearful leaders who are trying to play god.

For you and me, the stark bottom line is that God's sons should *expect* harsh treatment in this life, not be surprised when it comes, and rejoice that we are considered worthy of the same experience as our Savior. A worldly man does not get this, but God's Man does because he is, above all, a son of God and a brother to Jesus:

> In bringing many sons to glory, it was fitting that God, for whom and through whom everything exists, should make the author of their salvation perfect through suffering. Both the one who makes men holy and those who are made holy are of the *same family.* So Jesus is not ashamed to call them brothers. (Hebrews 2:10–11)

Key words: "same family."

That is a huge paradigm shift away from the gospel of comfort and convenience permeating the body of Christ today. It is a quantum departure from the "bless me" clubs of Christian men who are socializing comfortably while injustices and evil trample over innocent women and children worldwide. Sacrificial leadership in the face of hostility is so rare because it is only possible by a powerful, invisible, intangible inside God's Man.

It's spiritual man versus spiritual boy.

God does not ask you to take risks for Him without assurance or to believe in Him without real evidence. He indwells, inhabits, and infuses God's Man with an inner witness that substantiates your commitment to Christ while compelling bold, seemingly incongruent stands for Christ. Jesus's most powerful witness to us through the Holy Spirit comes in a hostile world: "Peace I leave with you; my peace I give you. I do not give to you as the world gives. Do not let your hearts be troubled and do not be afraid" (John 14:27).

Translation: You can be calm under pressure. Jesus contrasted how culture defined peace against the peace that the Holy Spirit would bring.

The world gives peace in the presence of comfort and in the absence of hardship or hostilities. You've seen the commercial: two people on a white, sandy beach as they sip beer to the sounds of the sleepy ocean tide. That's how the world brings peace. The defining marker is the absence of conflict.

The Holy Spirit, by contrast, brings peace in the midst of conflict, distress, and persecution. It simply doesn't make sense for the Comforter to

> *It simply doesn't make sense for the Comforter to bring comfort to the comfortable.*

bring comfort to the comfortable. Why would they need it? Reality says that comfort is most deeply felt and experienced in the midst of discomfort.

In a strange way, the more uncomfortable a circumstance or the risk for God, the more profoundly I experience the ministry of the Holy Spirit. For the sake of our discussion, it takes real courage to look for situations that create "helicopter gut," a visceral feeling in the pit of your stomach that is a combination of wonder and fear over a decision to do what God asks. The upside of moving against feelings or circumstances in faith is that those situations are when the Holy Spirit will be present and His power will explode.

There are some things you can only receive through the filter of your faith, and this is one of them. So I recommend that you run toward discomfort to find God. Nonsensical? *Yes.* Countercultural? *Probably.* Create an emotional fever? *Count on it.* But just like the shepherd-king David, once your Spirit-filled man hears it, your spiritual warrior is triggered. This will be the moment when other men are walking away, but you will be sprinting confidently toward the unknown in the power of the Holy Spirit.

Mighty warrior (that's you!), if you want to see what can happen, take these three steps.

Step 1: Pick a giant.

> Now it is God who makes both us and you stand firm in Christ. He anointed us, set his seal of ownership on us, and put his Spirit in our hearts as a deposit, guaranteeing what is to come. (2 Corinthians 1:21–22)

SOAR Principle: The Holy Spirit is in you to take the worry out of you as you face hostility or discomfort in your commitment to Christ.

You can stand firm and stand firm *in Him.* God indwelling you is your invisible intangible that will make you *stand and face* versus *turn and flee* the challenges in your life. So pick a giant and go after it! Your love for Christ, made powerful by the Holy Spirit, will dispatch your fear with each step forward.

Start walking toward the front lines.

Step 2: Get a guarantee.

> *God* himself has *prepared us* for this, and as *a guarantee* he has given us *his Holy Spirit.* So we are *always confident,* even though we know that as long as we live in

these bodies we are not at home with the Lord. For we *live by believing* and not by seeing. Yes, we are *fully confident,* and we would rather be away from these earthly bodies, for then we will be at home with the Lord. So whether we are here in this body or away from this body, our *goal is to please him.* (2 Corinthians 5:5–9, NLT)

SOAR Principle: A guarantee creates inner certainty.

In manworld we call it "walking tall." God wants every believer walking tall (like David) in the Spirit. The solution is to internalize versus intellectualize the guarantee and confidence the Holy Spirit exists to provide. With that goal in mind, the simplest way to manifest the presence of the Holy Spirit is by speaking the truth of Scripture into the moments that call for courage and confidence. It looks like this: the Word of Truth joins with the Spirit of Truth and faith in God joins with words of God, openly believed and spoken, to produce the power of God. With Jesus as our example throughout the New Testament, I offer you an exercise to practice this important spiritual discipline based on the scripture above. Join your faith with the Holy Spirit and repeat out loud the following:

The Creed of the Guaranteed

God has prepared me.

The Holy Spirit is in me.

Nothing can stop me.

Nothing can hurt me.

If God is for me.

Because HE will redeem me.

God wants us to practice reminding ourselves of spiritual truth on a daily and moment-by-moment basis. The purpose of this exercise is to connect you with truth.

God wants you to be inwardly certain and fully confident of the Holy Spirit's presence right now. More personally, God wants this truth and the confidence it engenders to fully sync up with your heart and not just your mind. The reason I asked you to recite this creed is because being certain of the Holy Spirit's presence is not an intellectual exercise; it is a spiritual and experiential reality that produces a real, living, and emotional validation of truth inside you. It is a combination of hearing truth, trusting truth, and embracing inward transformation. That's what you just did.

"What's the big deal?" you ask.

You will run into battle more aggressively if you know you can't lose! Then, and only then, do the arenas of battle, the issues, or the opponents become inconsequential. David's personal closeness to God drove his confidence in God. How certain inwardly was David? Watch the scrawny shepherd from Israel address the giant from Gath. Do you detect any doubt?

> **soar fact**
> *The inwardly certain man is the calm and confident man under pressure.*

> David said to the Philistine, "You come against me with sword and spear and javelin, but I come against you in the name of the LORD Almighty, the God of the armies of Israel, whom you have defied. This day the LORD will hand you over to me, and I'll strike you down and cut off your head. Today I will give the carcasses of the Philistine army to the birds of the air and the beasts of the earth, and the whole world will know that there is a God in Israel. All those gathered here will know that it is not by sword or spear that the LORD saves; for the battle is the LORD's, and he will give all of you into our hands." (1 Samuel 17:45–47)

Where did that come from? Answer: confidence springing from relationship, faith in God joining promises of God, openly believed and spoken. For the record, as David confidently predicted, the world did know just a few minutes later that everything he said was true.

Another example of such confidence came when a New Testament man, Peter, with his new guarantee of the Holy Spirit lodged deep within him, stared down the Goliaths who had crucified Jesus:

> Then Peter, filled with the Holy Spirit, said to them: "Rulers and elders of the people! If we are being called to account today for an act of kindness shown to a cripple and are asked how he was healed, then know this, you and all the people of Israel: It is by the name of Jesus Christ of Nazareth, whom you crucified but whom God raised from the dead, that this man stands before you healed....
>
> "Salvation is found in no one else, for there is no other name under heaven given to men by which we must be saved."
>
> When they saw the courage of Peter and John and realized that they were unschooled, ordinary men, they were astonished and they took note that these men had been with Jesus. (Acts 4:8–10, 12–13)

What do we see? The filled, fearless, faithful, fantastic confidence of the Spirit! God's Man is free to suffer or die because of the real indwelling guarantee of the Holy Spirit.

With spiritual confidence flooding the soul of God's Man, it's time to see God's real end game for the use of spiritual courage.

Step 3: Shock the world as God's Men.

> These men are not drunk, as you suppose. It's only nine in the morning! No, this is what was spoken by the prophet Joel:
> "In the last days, God says,
>   I will pour out my Spirit on all people.
> Your sons and daughters will prophesy,
>   your young men will see visions,
>   your old men will dream dreams.
> Even on my servants, both men and women,
>   I will pour out my Spirit in those days,
>   and they will prophesy.

I will show wonders in the heaven above
and signs on the earth below,
blood and fire and billows of smoke." (Acts 2:15–19)

When you encounter large pockets of men under the influence of the Holy Spirit, all moving in concert with the purposes of God on earth, they act like a cultural stun gun. In fact, their gathering is so atypical, distinctive, and countercultural, it has to be explained. People don't get it. It is not what they are used to seeing from the men in their culture. It defies any other explanation apart from an indisputable work of God.

> **soar fact**
> *The usual expression of the Holy Spirit is to ignite the unusual or unnatural from inside of men for all to see.*

I am seeing nonbelievers scratching their heads and being blown away by Spirit-formed and Spirit-filled men every day at Saddleback Church and around the world. Large pockets of men from my own church have recently taken over a two-hundred-room transitional homeless motel every weekend to serve food, connect with the marginalized, pray with and baptize new believers, and give dignity to the untouchables of our society. Result: the homeless of Santa Ana are being blown away by the men of the OC acting so strangely.

The Joshua Generation movement in Brazil is full of young God's Men who are saying no to sexual promiscuity in order to say yes to purity and respecting women. Result: the ladies of Brazil are shocked. The GLOVIMO (Glory in Virginity movement) men of Uganda are blowing the minds of their countrymen and significantly lowering the HIV infection rate in the power of the Spirit. Result: the world is shocked.

But God is not surprised a bit.

When the Holy Spirit is poured out on a body of men, it is nothing short of a spectacle. Think large flames, pillars of smoke, and a commotion of activity, with bystanders wondering and speculating what on earth is going on over there? Think serious power, like a massive natural gas explosion. But instead of people suffering in the blast zone of broken male culture, men under the influence of the Holy Spirit create a positive impact zone that leads to greater measures of life and health for those around them.

The entire sociology of nations, violence against women, violent crime, public health, political leadership, and the vibrancy of the family benefits from the powerful transformations ignited by the Holy Spirit among men. *KUH-BOOM!* Cultural men become God's Men and begin living differently.

In this respect, every man you see is a box of dynamite. Each one is the sleeping giant of the world who needs to be reached, activated with the good news, and transformed into a giant killer. As men come under the influence and ministry of the Holy Spirit, stuff happens—exciting stuff. Transformed men will bring revival, redemption, and a new release of Holy Spirit health globally. Their behaviors will transcend and dwarf the smallness of the cultural practices around them and ignite blast zones of life that will demand notice, threaten leaders, and *invite persecution,* because power always threatens power.

This is what Holy Spirit power flowing among men looks like: He transforms the former men into new leaders to do the new works of God that threaten the established and broken male culture around them. That is what happened to Peter and the disciples at Pentecost, and that is what transpired with the apostle Paul and his buddies. That's what always happens when groups of men aggressively seek the Lord, pray, open His Word, and make themselves willing to do anything He asks.

Here's an example:

> While they were worshiping the Lord and fasting, the Holy Spirit said, "Set apart for me Barnabas and Saul for the work to which I have called them." So after they had fasted and prayed, they placed their hands on them and sent them off. (Acts 13:2–3)

Want to see the Holy Spirit start setting off some explosions of the kingdom in your church and community? Connect with other men, invite the Holy Spirit to come and take over your fellowship, and earnestly seek the Lord's face through worship, fellowship, and discipleship. If you do this, anointed ministry and mission are sure to follow. The Holy Spirit will come. He will speak. He will call you to face the fear. He will guarantee your courage.

If that's your desire, pray this prayer as you run into battle today:

> *Holy Spirit, prepare me for the battle to come. Show me a Goliath in my life who needs to fall and move me to the front lines. Show me a sin that needs to fall and move me to the front lines. Show me a relationship that needs my attention and move me to the front lines. Show me a person who needs to meet Jesus today and move me to the front lines. Show me a mission I can perform for You in the midst of my time on earth and move me to the front lines. Show me an injustice among men that I can help right and move me to the front lines. Rise up in me. Rise up in my mind. Rise up in my heart. Rise up in my hands and feet. Rise up in my words. Take over the next days and months and years, and ignite the life of God through me.*
>
> *Jesus, I commit to You alone. Today I will stand for You by the power of the Holy Spirit. For Jesus' sake. Amen.*

bad physics

Problems seldom exist on the level at which they are expressed.

—KARE ANDERSON

Snapped like a twig.

As I stared at the glowing x-ray film of my son's upper arm, I couldn't believe how bad the break looked. My face was saying "Wow!" and "Ouch!" at the same time. Before me was the luminous skeletal shot of Ryan's right upper extremity, showing his collarbone, shoulder, and upper arm. Just imagine holding a tree branch against your knee and breaking the branch by force, leaving each hand with a piece of the now separated branch. The branch on the x-ray was Ryan's humerus (the long upper bone between your shoulder and your elbow). With that bone now broken in two, his arm was being held together by flesh, nerves, and tendons. The x-ray was a visceral, visual sucker punch that literally took my breath. Google "humerus bone," and you will see what I mean.

The day had begun with nine inches of fresh Utah powder, which presented us with a brilliant snowboarding opportunity. Ryan was only two runs into his day with the terrain providing the exact risks and opportunities he had been dreaming of: grinding rails, box features, and big air jumps. The key word is *air*. Not air to breathe, but air meaning to defy gravity.

For a snowboarder, getting air and landing safely is like when a surfer drops into a big wave, gets tubed, and emerges still standing. Such feats are intoxicating for the soul and make you want second and third helpings. Successful episodes are usually accompanied by smiles, fist pumping, triumphant squawking, and at the end of the day, tall tales. It's pure adrenaline and pure joy after a full swallow of athletic risk. I call it yummy danger, and no drug can compete with it. I got Ryan addicted to snowboarding when he was little, and we have been pushing the borders of our skills ever since.

That day, Ryan's first jump was a successful 180-degree turn in midair. He'd been building up to this and gaining more confidence to try it on a bigger stage, so the fact that he landed it out of the box was a huge rush. The rest of his story on the mountain that day was textbook. Naturally, success on jump number one leads to a desire for a second big air maneuver, but this time the physics (emotional and physical) were different all the way around:

- Too much confidence
- Too much speed
- Too little experience
- Too steep a jump
- Too much height
- Too much air for a novice jumper to handle

All these factors created extra bad physics, which made for a scary moment. Ryan dumped it on the other end of the jump like he had so many times in the past, but this time he didn't get up. The jump created too much vertical height and too little horizontal length. In other words, he fell off a roof!

When you are snowboarding, a good trajectory means a long, flat arch versus a short, high one. Since Ryan's mechanics bought him the latter, he hit the downside of the jump with his right arm at full force. Just imagine falling straight down in a horizontal or flat position and landing on some kind of an edge. It's awkward, unnatural, and disturbing to watch. This is the physics of density and impact. As Ryan put it, "I didn't think I was hurt at first, but when I tried to pull my arm in, and it wouldn't move, I knew I was in trouble."

The pain honeymoon didn't last long either, as the pain center in Ryan's brain flooded with signals. His hand started to go numb because of nerve damage around the break. We learned later that his radial nerve—which travels from the spinal cord, wraps itself around the humerus, and travels down to the hand—was damaged. He'd lost all feeling in his hand.

After two days of excruciating pain, Ryan had to have his bone reset by an orthopedic specialist. Practically, resetting the bone meant that the doctor had to grip both sides of the break, pull the bones apart, and then push them together again in order to ensure proper alignment of the bone.

Oh, joy.

That day and the resetting memory are seared into Ryan's brain like the mark of a hot branding iron—it's permanent because of the powerful dose of pain that went with it. After this torture, he was fitted with a special brace and then x-rayed weekly for the next five weeks. All this effort was necessary to make sure the bone was acceptably aligned, so proper healing could take place. The one upside was that the bone would grow back stronger in the location of the break. Go figure: massive break, huge pain, and you wind up with a *stronger* bone!

So what do bad physics, bad breaks, x-rays, painful realignments, and the healing process have to do with your relationship with the Holy Spirit?

Everything.

You will

- fracture it.
- lose function.
- lose movement in your spiritual life.
- need to treat it.
- need to look at it from the inside out.
- need to reset it.

- need to heal it.
- need to grow it back stronger in the place of injury.
- need to analyze it so the injury doesn't happen again.

> ## soar fact
> *There is no other relationship in the life of a Christian that needs to be as aggressively protected and guarded as the connection with the Holy Spirit. It supports the entire life in God.*

Broken bones and broken relationships have a ton in common. The Bible tells us *in advance* what the spiritual physics of a bad break with the Holy Spirit look like. Fortunately, we also are told how to find healing in the unfortunate event of a break.

Holy Spirit Fractures

A Christian's relationship to the Holy Spirit is largely unseen.

How many believers have you encountered who gave the appearance that everything was solidly put together on the outside, but inside their life was full of pain from relational, moral, spiritual, and emotional traumas? After thousands of counseling sessions, so often what I see underneath is an undiagnosed or untreated spiritual fracture in a person's relationship with the Holy Spirit. The believer and the Spirit of God are not connected, and by default, that person loses the functional power of his spiritual life to help him grow, change, heal, and experience health in his relationships with God and people. In the same way Ryan lost the function of his right arm on the slopes of Utah, these men try to move things forward, but they just don't have the inner strength and structure to do it. For them, ignorance incapacitates.

After this orthopedic episode and season with Ryan, I *now know* that, based on the location of the break, there are three different types of humerus fractures: proximal, midshaft, and distal. Proximal is near the shoulder, midshaft is near the center of the upper arm, and distal is closer to the elbow joint. On an x-ray, they are easy to see.

I highlighted the fact that I "now know" because I find that many believers are ignorant of what spiritual fractures actually look like when it comes to their relationship with the Holy Spirit. All believers need to know the three different ways fellowship with the Holy Spirit can be broken. They are easy to identify and revolve around simple dynamics that put any relationship in jeopardy.

The good news for us believers is that, regardless of the severity of the spiritual fracture, this powerful relationship can be reset and realigned. Like the broken bone in our upper arm, the Holy Spirit has not been removed. He is still inside our physical body, still being held together by the structure of faith, and still holding the potential to powerfully heal us and make us spiritually stronger than we were before.

In your relationship with the Holy Spirit, there are three actions you want to avoid at all costs. I will name them and illustrate each with Scripture.

1. Lying to the Holy Spirit

> Now a man named Ananias, together with his wife Sapphira, also sold a piece
> of property. With his wife's full knowledge he kept back some of the money for
> himself, but brought the rest and put it at the apostles' feet.
>   Then Peter said, "Ananias, *how is it that Satan has so filled your heart that*
> *you have lied to the Holy Spirit* and have kept for yourself some of the money
> you received for the land? Didn't it belong to you before it was sold? And after
> it was sold, wasn't the money at your disposal? What made you think of doing
> such a thing? *You have not lied to men but to God.*" (Acts 5:1–4)

What was the Holy Spirit up to? Simply put: He was causing a holy commotion. Like a full-term mother delivering a baby, the Holy Spirit's job was to give birth to a healthy church. Beginning with the disciples, and then outward toward the people in Jerusalem, He was filling people full of salvation and transformation, just as Jesus had predicted. He was delivering powerful messages through the apostles. He was moving people to serve others in radical ways.

Many people were impressed by the Holy Spirit to give financially to meet the needs of others. One of the easier ways was to sell land and to give the proceeds to the apostles, who then distributed the money to those in need. Enter Ananias and his wife, Sapphira. They were witnessing all of this sharing, saw all of the attention givers were receiving, got caught up in all the excitement, and decided to get in on this visible philanthropy. In the process, they reasoned they would become visible themselves. Like many believers, they were doing the right thing with the wrong motives. More bluntly, they were pimping God for personal attention! Their love of attention and money were being fueled under the pretext of generosity. So through Peter, God outed Ananias and his wife to prevent them from polluting God's work.

Game up.

We lie to the Holy Spirit when, with full knowledge, we hijack God's purposes to fulfill our own needs. Lying to the Holy Spirit manifests itself in the form of subtle self-trickery, twisted logic, deception of others, and cooperation with Satan. For Ananias and Sapphira, it was not about God at all. It was all about appearances and playing church to project an image. The lengths they were willing to go to extend this charade were mind boggling, but their thinking had become so polluted, they had successfully compartmentalized and rationalized their behavior into a morally swallowable form. In the process, they mocked God, embezzled His glory (by taking it for themselves), and used His work as a means for social and financial advancement.

This all sounds strikingly similar to a certain fallen angel who was outed by God for the exact same reasons. (You can read more about him in my book *Fight*.) Peter saw Satan's fingerprints all over this crime scene and indicted him on the spot. In this instance, lying to the Holy Spirit was nothing short of a spiritual Ponzi scheme à la Bernie Madoff.

When I think of Ananias and Sapphira's story, I am reminded of clergy who proclaim Christ publicly but privately use their position to take advantage of the weak or vulnerable. I think of men who misuse Scripture in order to dominate their wives or abuse them physically, all in the name of biblical submission. I think of Christians who love to quote Scripture in order to make themselves feel more superior in the name of educating the less wise. I think about dudes who list "Christian" on their Facebook profile insincerely in order to connect with women and use them sexually. I think about believers who gossip under the banner of "she needs our prayers." I think of network marketers who care more about using the social networks of churches to get rich than to actually serve in that same church. I think of Christians who take cash advances on God's forgiveness, cheapening His grace, in order to dive into a sin they will confess and repent of later.

I think of how I, too, have been played by Satan and have pridefully taken the bait and used my faith for selfish purposes. Only by the grace of God am I alive today to tell you this, perhaps to cause you to think more seriously about what it means to be a Christian. At some level I think all of us can identify with Ananias and Sapphira. We all have talked ourselves into actions (seen and unseen) in the name of God that we come to regret.

One more time: *we lie to the Holy Spirit when we wear the mask of faith in order to deliver pleasure, satisfaction, or approval to our flesh.* This behavior will sever your fellowship with the Holy Spirit in a nanosecond because, as the Spirit of Truth, His character will not allow Him to empower deception of any kind.

To prevent this from happening and maintain a strong connection with the Holy Spirit, we must practice aggressive self-management and constantly ask ourselves:

- Why am I really doing this?
- What's my motive?
- Who gets the credit?
- Who benefits?
- Who's most encouraged?

This is called healthy self-reflection, or taking a spiritual inventory.

Finally, we must also present ourselves to God for a spiritual x-ray. An easy way to do this is to simply pray the words of Psalm 139:23–24. It is the equivalent of a spiritual heart scan and a powerful way to put your motives through security. Listen to David's words: "Search me, O God, and know my heart; test me and know my anxious thoughts. See if there is any offensive way in me, and lead me in the way everlasting."

God's Man prevents spiritual fractures through open submission and surrender to examination by God. He does a spiritual MRI to get to the bottom of his heart. Some of us need to put on our spiritual hospital gown, humble ourselves, and get checked out. It's uncomfortable, exposes our spiritual backside, and leaves us wondering what will come back on the film. But that's the price we pay for a relationship we value.

Meanwhile, don't take the bait. Don't accept the evil logic. Don't pretend or pose. Don't rationalize away your faith out of fear or for a feeling.

Don't lie to the Holy Spirit.

2. Grieving the Holy Spirit

Do not let any unwholesome talk come out of your mouths, but only what is helpful for building others up according to their needs, that it may benefit those who listen. *And do not grieve the Holy Spirit of God, with whom you were sealed for the day of redemption.* Get rid of all bitterness, rage and anger, brawling and slander, along with every form of malice. Be kind and compassionate to one another, forgiving each other, just as in Christ God forgave you. (Ephesians 4:29–32)

The Holy Spirit's best work in people is seen in how He changes the way they relate to one another. You want the best parts of your character displayed in your kids. When your positive qualities, ways, words, actions, and encouragements are reproduced in your child's interactions with others, that brings you joy. On the opposite end, though, if they abuse, discourage, and harm others by their words and ways, that brings you grief. "That's not me!" you protest. I think our waywardness has the same effect on the Holy Spirit.

One of the Holy Spirit's tasks is to experientially validate for every believer God's awesome love, acceptance, and encouragement toward each of His children. We "taste and see" that the Lord is good through the Holy Spirit, bringing His goodness to us (see Psalm 34:8). We sense it and feel it deeply. We love how the Holy Spirit takes the intellectual concepts of the love, mercy, and grace of God and makes them practical and experiential.

But it's not supposed to stop there, my brotha. The real end game is that we give away that same affirmation, acceptance, forgiveness, encouragement, and support to others in our arenas of influence—beginning with our own family. Versus what? Tearing people down with our words, holding on to resentments, and practicing vengeance. One is the work of the Holy Spirit in and through a believer; the other is the work of evil in and through a believer.

In the Holy Spirit's framework, it is incongruent for a grace-receiving sinner to become an anger-delivering destroyer. Only a man who has forgotten his own encounter with God's grace could deny it intentionally to someone else. No believer can claim a close fellowship with the Holy Spirit while acting out of anger, bitterness, and resentment toward someone else. One cannot be a party to the other. Only a spiritual con man who's had a mountain of debt forgiven by God would try to squeeze emotional nickels out of another through a lack of forgiveness.

> **soar fact**
> *The Holy Spirit heals relationships. He does this by leading and prompting all believers to show to others what God has shown them in the person of Christ.*

Jesus aggressively illustrated His heart on this matter in the parable of the unmerciful servant (see Matthew 18:23–35). His point: you didn't deserve grace, but now that you have it, you better give it as liberally as you received it! If we don't, the same thing grieves the Holy Spirit.

All of us, by honestly and sincerely saying a prayer, can restore spiritual equilibrium in this area. This prayer acknowledges that, in spite of our best intentions, we can sadden and disappoint the Holy Spirit. Pray this prayer as a simple realignment or if a relationship is challenging you in the area of forgiveness:

Holy Spirit, thank You for helping me feel God's grace, mercy, and acceptance. I am sorry for not reproducing this experience more in my relationships with others. I don't want to grieve You by being greedy with Your grace. I want God's grace to flow to me and through me.

Remind me of the Cross. Remind me of the blood that flowed down the head, down the back, down the arms, down the sides, down the feet of Jesus, so that I could be forgiven. Remind me of my mission on earth to be an agent of that same grace. Help me to let go of resentments early and trade them in for Your grace.

Make me an encourager like You, building others up in simple ways. With my wife. With my children. With those not like me. With those You will bring into my life today. As You heal me with God's grace and love, explode that healing out of me to heal my relationships. I don't want to grieve You. I want just to please You. Amen.

3. Putting Out the Spirit's Fire

Be joyful always; pray continually; give thanks in all circumstances, for this is God's will for you in Christ Jesus.

Do not put out the Spirit's fire; do not treat prophecies with contempt. Test everything. Hold on to the good. Avoid every kind of evil. (1 Thessalonians 5:16–22)

As we have learned, the Holy Spirit is a drawing and inviting presence for believers and through believers to others. Picture a warm fire, and imagine its glow and radiating heat bringing all around it calm and comfort. If you see that picture, you are getting close to the experience that the Holy Spirit wants to create for you and for others through you! Now go back to that fire and imagine this: some dude cruises in and douses your bonfire with a five-gallon bucket of water! What feelings would rise up inside you? What would you say? What would you do?

When we look at the Scripture passage carefully, we see three ways the fire of God is stoked or extinguished in our life. The fire stokers would include all expressions of worship, talking to God about all matters in all moments of life, and an attitude of gratitude. These act like a highly flammable spiritual accelerant in your journey with

God, and the Holy Spirit will prompt you to practice all three as a way of life to keep His fire burning hot.

On the other side, the fire extinguishers would include an uncooperative spirit, an unteachable spirit, and an easily diverted spirit (verses 19–21). Instead of being a partner with the Holy Spirit's work in us, we become like a rebellious and adversarial adolescent. Instead of joining His works in the world through our involvement, we make excuses for not participating. Instead of hungering for more revelation of God's Word, we act like we have it wired and pridefully deflect the fresh manna served up by the Holy Spirit. Instead of recognizing the spiritual war for our soul and filtering what we let into our mind, we adopt cultural ways of thinking and blend them with our faith. We are *all* tempted in these ways; otherwise the admonitions wouldn't be there!

Every day (actually, this is a moment-to-moment choice) we will either be a fire stoker of the Holy Spirit's work in and through us or be a fire extinguisher of His work. Habits that serve to throw spiritual gas on the fire would definitely include

- meditation on the Word of God.
- application of the Word of God.
- assimilation of prayer toward growth in character and conduct.
- connections and confession with other believers.
- willingness to receive correction.
- service toward others.
- encouragement of other believers.
- evangelization of nonbelievers.

The Spirit-formed, -filled, and -fired life involves these "hot habits."

How important is the Holy Spirit's work to you? If it is not important, you are automatically an obstacle. Do not put out the Spirit's fire. Don't let it die.

Stoke it!

Holy Spirit, You are a fire that wants to spread in me and through me in the world. I am done being an obstacle! Show me how I extinguish the fire of God that wants to roar through my issues. Consume them and create a new person out of the ashes. Show me the lives You want to set ablaze and use me to stoke and kindle the fire in them. Show me situations where Your fire may be dying and You want to use me to stoke it back to life through Your power. Fuel Your fire in me through the simple spiritual habits of soaking in Your Word and igniting its power in my life through prayer. Consume me, Holy Spirit, today. Make me Your holy fire, for Jesus' sake. Amen.

Part 2

transformations

the welcomed interruption

Bosom up my counsel, you'll find it wholesome.
　　　　—WILLIAM SHAKESPEARE, *The Life of King Henry VIII*

Meet Vijay (vee-jay).

You may not know that name, but he is as famous as they come in the little fishing village of Nallavadu on the Indian coast. Vijay, a native of this small coastal community, happened to be in Singapore for a science congress when the tsunami of the century struck all of Southeast Asia in the early morning hours of December 26, 2004. Fifty-eight minutes after midnight that day, the seafloor off the coast of Sumatra, Indonesia, subducted and fell beneath another ocean plate to create the largest earthquake ever recorded. This collision of the earth's crust and the subsequent 9.3 magnitude earthquake vaulted walls of water as high as one hundred feet toward eleven countries bordering the Indian Ocean.

If you weren't directly exposed to it, it is tough to get your arms around the size and scale of such a natural phenomenon. Just imagine a sumo wrestler weighing over three hundred pounds jumping into a small kiddie pool. You get the picture. The whole event (earthquake and tsunami) will end only after things get hit. It is a massive displacement of water moving outward from the point of origin with progressively increasing force.

And the farther it travels, the larger it gets.

Monitors in Indonesia had registered the movement caused by the mammoth quake in the early morning hours, but of course everyone was asleep. At the worst, Vijay may have felt a gentle nudge or bump in the night. All Singapore residents were blissfully ignorant that this modest rolling and shaking was the harbinger of a titanic horror now making its deadly journey toward them across open seas. Natural disasters typically don't announce themselves, so most of the time all you can do is react. But Vijay's location allowed him the rare opportunity to help others east of him react *before* the tsunami's landfall would devastate their homes.

> *Natural disasters typically don't announce themselves.*

———

Sunday, December 26, 2004. Sunrise.

Vijay's biological clock goes off. After a long, intense stretch, he opens his eyes, takes a big deep breath, and wills his body to stand. The bathroom beckons. Mission accomplished, he hits the "On" button on the radio to keep him company while he gets ready for work. It's a familiar routine going on all over Singapore at this hour. One press of the button today, however, and any idea of normal goes out the window. Something is wrong.

"That's not my station! Wait. What's the man saying?"

Vijay stops brushing his teeth and turns up the radio. He is mesmerized by what he hears.

"Can't be," he says to himself.

His ears begin to assimilate and assemble the words coming over the shortwave about how a natural disaster is unfolding in real time all over Southeast Asia. Words begin to register and connect: *earthquake, magnitude 9.3, tsunami, coast of Singapore, unconfirmed reports, thousands missing, coastal communities on the Indian peninsula in imminent danger.* His mind struggles to process all these grave realities when suddenly he realizes, *The television! Turn on the television! Vijay, it's happening right now!*

It is all over the news, and the initial footage is surreal. "Tsunami" flashes across the bottom of his television screen. Aerial footage of Singapore's coastline reveals the devastation caused by a massive wall of water. The footage is vivid and fresh, but the details are sketchy. The news reporter is visibly shaken and keeps repeating what she knows.

Vijay's mind is reeling, and then, eerily, calm and clarity come over him. He can feel a deep uneasiness and nausea beginning to gnaw at his stomach as a revelation is brought to light, a connection, a gathering of his senses, a coalescing of unfolding events, an uninvited vision of the future. He sees his father pushing his small fishing boat out to sea in India. That thought bounces out and another takes its place. *Didn't the news say the tsunami was headed toward India?*

The vision is crippling. A quick look at his watch and his chest tightens. More images of home. It would be business as usual back in Nallavadu. In just about an hour the village fishermen will put out to sea as they always do, trolling the coastal waters for the daily catch. Back on shore the rest of his family and close friends would be setting about their tasks without a care under sunny skies. And by the end of this same hour, the eastbound tsunami would slam into all of them.

While his vision is grave, the reality far surpasses it. For at the exact moment Vijay realizes the impending fate of his father, family, and friends, marine technicians tracking the killer wave discover that their communications system for warning countries in harm's way is inoperative because of the quake. Vijay does not know this. Later it would be learned that no combination of events (earthquake, tsunami, and communication breakdown) has ever coalesced to kill more people *in one day* in recorded history: nearly a quarter of a million people will die.

Vijay's heart rate spikes and he labors to breathe. Adrenaline rushes. What happens next is a miracle in the midst of a massacre.

A reporter from Malaysia was the first to discover a silver lining to the tragic day. She wrote later about Vijay:

> He decided to phone home.
>
> His sister answered the phone. She told him that seawater was seeping into their home when he asked what was happening in Nallavadu. Vijayakumar realized at once that his worst fears were rapidly materializing. He asked his sister to quickly leave their home and to also warn other villagers to evacuate the village. "Run out and shout the warning to others," he urged his sister.
>
> Her warning reached a couple of quick-thinking villagers who broke down the doors of the community centre set up by the M S Swaminathan Research Foundation where a public address system used routinely to announce sea conditions to the fishermen was housed. The warning from Vijayakumar was broadcast across the village using the loudspeaker system. The village's siren was sounded immediately afterwards for the people to evacuate.
>
> No one was killed in this village as a result of the timely warnings. Nallavadu is home to 500 families and about 3,630 people. While all lives were saved, the tsunami destroyed 150 houses and 200 fishing boats in the village.[1]

Did you catch that? "Timely warnings.... All lives were saved."

Upon hearing the warning, each villager started moving in a new direction: away from shore and toward the refuge of higher ground. Only in that region could life be preserved and peace secured in the face of inevitable and impending danger.

Sadly, neighboring villages not fortunate enough to receive a warning call were overwhelmed. Life and peace were shattered in an instant and replaced with panic, then chaos and death. Hundreds perished while Vijay's thousands lived. In this moment he became for his people a well-placed, well-timed, well-intentioned, and *welcomed* interruption. Few men will ever be given the opportunity and ability to dramatically help so many others in so short a time. Then again, few men in history will actually be able *to see the future before it happens.*

———

Vijay was an unlikely hero, or perhaps an accidental hero. But in the end, he was in the right place at the right time, and he did the right thing to help save others from certain death. Regardless of what we call him, the people he warned call him a savior. This is what you call a person who follows a pattern of thinking and acting similar to what a savior does:

- He foresees harm to people.
- He is in a unique position to intervene.
- He is willing to intervene.
- He acts to make contact and warn.
- He interjects himself into and interrupts the lives of others.
- He warns, informs, and gives specific details of a coming danger.
- He guides and shows how to avoid death.
- He prompts movement in a new direction.
- He saves many from inevitable chaos and death.
- His actions are used to bring life, safety, and peace to those who heed his warning.

Oh, I almost forgot. The "no time to spare" factor magnifies every one of these factors—every emotion, every second, and every decision—a hundredfold for both the savior and those who would be saved. Think about it: a magnitude 9.3 earthquake, a giant tsunami, thousands of people unaware, and one man able to make a difference. And not one lost life resulted.

If this real-life drama sounds familiar, you are catching my drift! This story mirrors the role and function of the Holy Spirit in our life when He speaks as well as how we should embrace His message. Vijay spoke and everyone listened promptly. The same should be true with the Holy Spirit and us. The context of the crisis afforded Vijay the strongest possible voice. In the same way, the Holy Spirit's voice of authority should intersect our crossroads and crises. Here's why:

Positional Authority. Vijay's firsthand knowledge of unfolding events and his vantage point from Singapore empowered him with authority. He was a reliable source of information. His knowledge and location also authorized and allowed him to command and give orders without being questioned. His leverage was in the facts of what was happening. This is the Holy Spirit in your life at this second. He is both in it and above it and able to see what you can't and know what you don't. He has valuable, life-saving intel for you that no one else possesses. So since He alone has the skinny on your life and has your best interests in mind, listen up, homey!

Relational Authority. Vijay's closeness to his sister and the people he was warning was rock solid. "Hey, it's me, Vijay. I need you to listen very carefully to me right now. There is no time." It's called relational proximity. Think about your own brother or sister talking to you like that over the phone. How would you react? Vijay's leverage was his *close connection.* The Holy Spirit is the indwelling Christ. It can't get any closer than that! Whatever emotional attachment, loyalty, or relationship you have with Jesus is experienced through the Holy Spirit's presence in your life. Get that! He is the reason you feel close to God. He is the reason you sense the presence of God. He is the reason you are able to defeat sin, win at relationships, and change. The two of you have a lot of history and proximity. When He says, "Hey, it's Me," lean in!

Experiential Authority. Not only is experience the best teacher, it is the best persuader. Vijay had been actively involved with and was now on the other side of an event that was about to be repeated elsewhere in the region. There is no substitute for "I was just there" or "We've been hit, it's coming your way, and here's what you need to do." People usually don't argue with the voice of experience. Vijay's leverage was his personal exposure to events soon to become their future. The Holy Spirit is *both* before and after every event in your life. When He speaks to you, He is the voice of experience from age to age. He's been around, managed a few billion lives, and seen it all. You don't push back when a Person like this speaks. You just listen, take in the message, and do what He leads you to do. You trust His leadership and direction implicitly...and act quickly.

> *The Holy Spirit does not sway people without the positional authority knowledge gives, the relational authority a strong connection gives, and the experiential authority knowledge of the future gives.*

The Holy Spirit does not sway people without the positional authority knowledge gives, the relational authority a strong connection gives, and the experiential authority knowledge of the future gives. Without those, we will question any voice, and what they say will be open to interpretation. It's called lacking credibility.

Look at Vijay again. He had it all: he achieved 100 percent trust, resulting in 100 percent compliance, resulting in zero loss of life. Reflect on that: *zero loss.* It wasn't the government talking. It wasn't some unknown alarmist getting worked up on the Internet. And it wasn't some scientist espousing theories about how events might play out. It was *Vijay.* No other voice in that moment could be trusted more to lead his villagers out of danger and to safety.

Likewise, when your life, relationships, future, personal issues, and progress are on the line, no other voice has more authority, is more trustworthy, or is more right on *for you* than the Holy Spirit. You cannot lose. *Zero losses.*

A nonresponse to the Holy Spirit in those crucial life moments would be unthinkable.

Oh, by the way, don't expect to hear the Holy Spirit speak into your selections off a dinner menu or tell you what shoes to wear. He might, but in my experience, it's the moral, spiritual, relational, and emotional conflicts where He is most active.

> **soar fact**
> *The Holy Spirit works to interrupt a process and influence your thinking in contexts that will impact your relationships with God and people.*

A Saving Voice Needs a Willing Mind

Warning and saving. Influence and authority. Life and death.

These are some of the dynamics in play when a believer considers how to relate to the Holy Spirit on a more personal and functional level.

God's Man always runs the risk of being pimped by his old nature, old voices, old ways of thinking, and old ways of dealing with life, all of which were separate from the Spirit's control. Any of us can be broken down culturally, physically, emotionally, relationally, or spiritually and begin to think self-destructively. Thankfully, though, the moments that really challenge us are the ones that can grow us a spiritual spine. Think of Jesus in the Garden of Gethsemane or Joseph in that Egyptian jail. These are the times when Holy Spirit strength is waiting and poised to invade our weakness and bring God's perspective, purpose, and power to our upside-down and counterintuitive predicaments. In these moments we must choose the Holy Spirit's direction over the easier, better feeling, or more convenient and comfortable dark impulses that beckon for indulgence. It's called *sacrificing for a higher allegiance*. It's called becoming a man. It's called being Christlike. It's called activating Holy Spirit power.

> *The battlefield lesson is this: if we don't have a mind-set to please God before our challenges hit, it will be difficult to side with the Spirit of God in the middle of such testing.*

Every God's Man experiences these valleys and pits, but not every man succumbs to his self-destructive sinful nature at the expense of his connection to the Holy Spirit. The battlefield lesson is this: if we don't have a mind-set to please God before our challenges hit, it will be difficult to side with the Spirit of God in the middle of such testing. Practically, this means making up our mind *in advance* to side with the Spirit when the chips are down and the pressure is on. This predetermined choice, which eliminates bad options in the heat of the moment, is called a willing mind.

Look at the apostle Paul's definition of living according to the Holy Spirit in his foundational message to the believers in Rome:

> Those who live according to the sinful nature have their minds set on what that nature desires; but those who live in accordance with the Spirit have their *minds set* on what the Spirit desires. The mind of sinful man is death, but the mind controlled by the Spirit is life and peace. (Romans 8:5–6)

Translation: Focus in advance on what the Holy Spirit wants. God's Man knows that when he listens promptly to the Spirit's saving voice, he is spared the pain, panic, and loss that come from listening to the sultry voices of the dark side within.

Listen to a dad telling a son about the mental posture God is looking for and where the battle for his relationship with God is really won:

> And you, my son Solomon, acknowledge the God of your father, and serve
> him with wholehearted devotion and with *a willing mind,* for the LORD
> searches every heart and understands every motive behind the thoughts.
> (1 Chronicles 28:9)

Translation: Son, don't play games with God. That's a zero-sum game. He doesn't weigh actions. He measures intentions. Be willing in advance to do what He says.

God wants to know if you are going through the motions right now or if you are with Him body *and* spirit! He really wants to know if you are with Him at the heart level. Inner allegiance was a priority to Jesus for anyone claiming to follow Him: "These people honor *me* with their lips, but their *hearts are far from me*" (Matthew 15:8).

Listen to God describe the core disposition that He loves so much in a man and the spiritual life that it reflects out in the open:

> After removing Saul, [God] made David their king. He testified concerning
> him: "I have found David son of Jesse a man after my own heart; he will do
> everything I want him to do." (Acts 13:22)

Translation: God's Man is all in. Nothing is off the table. Better yet, God does not hide His enthusiasm for a son who is willing to be flexible and obedient, no matter what he asks.

At the center of your relationship with the Holy Spirit is a willingness to listen that rises above all other competing voices. That's what we call a friend of God.

While pain can be an effective catalyst for openness to input from the Holy Spirit, it is not nearly as good as desire and willingness. In any type of meaningful relationship, there must be a desire on the other side to commit, connect, learn, and listen.

I trust you see by now that the Holy Spirit is looking for a real relationship. This is seen by your willing submission to His voice and authority in your moment-by-moment peanut-butter-and-jelly life.

Keep reminding yourself: *He is a person.* He knows and can sense the difference between willing cooperation by a man and compliance. One is "want to" connect and relate; the other is "have to" comply. There's a huge difference. The Holy Spirit's voice should be a *welcomed, needed,* and *respected* interruption for us, no matter the situation, issue, or moment. Being disposed and ready to listen means increasing measures of life and peace for God's Man. Resenting, ignoring, or muting His voice results in chaos and destruction personally, spiritually, emotionally, and relationally.

The enemy of God and man (read my book *Fight* for much more on this topic) puts great energy into persuading you to *not* think in these terms. God's thinking on your relationship with the Holy Spirit is straightforward: "Since we live by the Spirit, let us keep in step with the Spirit" (Galatians 5:25). God's Man cannot afford to play nickel poker with the Holy Spirit when the stakes

soar fact
The Holy Spirit is an interrupting voice that comes between you and really bad choices.

are life and death. That is why all of us must face the control issues in our lives honestly, squarely, and biblically. We simply must ask, Who's in control? The answer is either (a) self or (b) the Holy Spirit.

God wants an answer to the question, Are you with Me? Give Him the nod now. And keep nodding!

I have one more point to make concerning your understanding of the Holy Spirit. Going back to Vijay's story, imagine this response from his sister when he called home with the warning of the approaching tsunami: "Thanks for the input, brother. I've heard what you said, but I'll take all that under advisement."

Under the circumstances we'd laugh and say, "Yeah, right." Why? Because that would be the equivalent of committing suicide. When the stakes are that high, you don't get to pick and choose your facts. How could anyone be so foolish? But how many times have we been stopped in our tracks by a thought or voice inside, reminded of who we are in Christ, and called to change direction only to press the "Mute" button on the Holy Spirit so that we can preserve our present course? Not you? Well, it's definitely me!

Maybe you can relate to this dynamic. When I want, I don't want to think. When my mind is made up, I have a direction and a set of expectations. I don't want anyone slowing down my process or hindering me from getting what I want. It's called having your mind made up "come hell or high water." That is why we have to make a commitment to God's will in advance of our day-to-day battles and in a strong way frequently and privately with Him. My impulsive decisions are not my best; they usually give me a hangover of conscience.

> *My point is this: commit to siding with the Holy Spirit every day— as in immediately after your eyes pop open in the morning. When we commit to Him before our battles, we partner better in our battles to be God's Man.*

My point is this: commit to siding with the Holy Spirit every day—as in immediately after your eyes pop open in the morning. When we commit to Him before our battles, we partner better in our battles to be God's Man. That's what it means to "keep in step with the Spirit" in Galatians 5:25. You line up and surrender daily. Do that, and you sell out less to your flesh.

Each step of the way, the goal should be to personalize the Holy Spirit in your life. With greater trust, comfort, and interaction, you will deepen not only your knowledge of Him but also your familiarity with His intentions and rhythms of interaction. Practically, we want to relate and connect with Him increasingly as a person, allowing Him to speak to us with loving authority, as Jesus told us He would: "He will bring glory to me by taking from what is mine and making it known to you" (John 16:14).

The difficulty for all believers is to take the step of faith and begin to relate to Him as a real person. Quite literally this means speaking to, praying to, and relating to the Holy Spirit in an intimate way. We can take comfort in the fact that even Jesus's disciples wrestled with getting functional with the Holy Spirit. But with Jesus not present on earth, we must push forward to a new relationship with Jesus vis-à-vis the Holy Spirit—just as the disciples did. And like them, with Jesus physically absent, we will go further with our commitment and service to God than ever before.

God is calling you to press into His person.

To do this, I have to remind myself daily of this personal dynamic. I remind myself that He is *not* an energy. He is *not* a personification of good qualities. He is *not* a force. He *is* an individual. He has specific things He wants to tell me. He has comfort and counsel He wants to give me. He wants to love and be loved back. He wants to be acknowledged for who He is. He gets sad and rejoices in my choices, like any friend would. He wants to be a saving voice and dominant influence in my life in order to give me more "life and peace" (Romans 8:6).

With all that is happening in you and around you, there is no room for a missed or dropped call with the Holy Spirit. As the commercial for the popular wireless carrier declares, we need more bars in more places, signaling a strong connection.

Here is a prayer you can pray to the Holy Spirit right now, allowing Him new access to your mind, willingly giving Him permission to interrupt, counsel, guide, and lead you away from self-destruction and selfish impulses and toward new places of growth and relationship. Pray with me:

> *Holy Spirit, I want You to be a saving voice in my life. There are so many things*
> *You are able to see that I cannot. There is so much that You know that I don't know.*

You are before and after all the issues in my life. I trust Your vantage point and wisdom. You are above my life, able to direct me, and guide me. Forgive me for thinking I can bring myself to safe places of life and peace in my own power.

I need Your warnings in my life as well as Your influence. I want You to have the strongest possible voice in my life. So right now I commit in advance to what You desire in my life. I make it my goal to please You at all times. I am looking forward to hearing You speak directly to my mind concerning God's will for my life. I am listening. Your friend, _____. Amen.

eyesight is insight

Nothing is more terrible than activity without insight.

—THOMAS CARLYLE

"So that's what 'blond' looks like…"

Those were the words of Mike May upon seeing his wife after forty-three years of blindness. No lie. What a line. What a journey. What a surreal moment for a man who had lost his eyesight at the age of three in the family garage when a freak chemical explosion scarred the corneas of both eyes and robbed him of his vision.

After four failed cornea replacement surgeries, Mike had spent most of his life accepting his blindness, getting acclimated to it, but refusing to be limited by it. He actually felt happy and fulfilled, despite being blind, because his life was atypical for any man, much less a blind man.

A short list of Mike's experiences before his world was turned upside-down by the recovery of his vision included:

- working for the CIA.
- founding his own electronics company.
- setting the world record for fastest downhill skiing speed by a blind person (65 mph).

- winning three gold medals at the Paralympic Games.
- carrying the Olympic torch on its way to Sarajevo for the 1984 Winter Olympics.
- speaking internationally.
- marrying a blond beauty.
- having and raising two boys.

Mike's achievements were embarrassingly spectacular! In fact, other blind people were so taken aback by his happiness in his blindness that they took offense. This was a case of the blind *shooting* the blind! None of this mattered that much to Mike, though, because he was enjoying his blind life to the fullest. And then seeing messed up everything!

While attending a conference in San Francisco, Mike's wife, Jennifer, discovered she needed some contacts, so she got the name of an ophthalmologist and scheduled an appointment. Mike tagged along, and when Jennifer entered the exam room to get fitted for her contacts, he went with her. Jennifer's exam was routine, but the situation turned surreal for Mike.

After finishing with Jennifer and writing a prescription for her contacts, the doctor caught a view of Mike's face and particularly his eye posture. Unable to resist, he asked the unsuspecting blind man, "Mind if I take a look?"

As a joke, Mike moved over to the ophthalmoscope and said, "I think you'll find that I am blind!"

After adjusting the scope to peer into Mike's eye, that is exactly what the doctor saw: massive corneal scarring. No big surprises. Then, oddly, after the quick assessment, came a second question: "Mind if my partner takes a look?"

Puzzled and curious, Mike agreed. He thought, *What is this about?* Mike heard a muffled conversation in the hallway.

Several minutes later, a second physician entered the exam room, introduced himself, and sat down in front of the scope. After examining Mike's eyes for a minute or two, he dropped a bomb: "Despite your horrible injury, there's good potential for vision in one of your eyes. I think it can benefit from a stem cell transplant. Mike, I think we can make you see."

Two surgeries later, Mike did just that.[2]

Staggering!

Mike's amazing surgery is called ocular surface reconstruction, and it connects directly to our discussion of the Holy Spirit. But first, here are the factoids on the procedure. I have highlighted the key dynamics:

1. Take *donor* stem cells that naturally occur in the eye (that is, not from the patient).
2. *Develop* sheets of them in the lab.
3. *Transplant* them onto the surface of the eye.
4. Hold these in place until they *fuse* with the eye.
5. The new cells *trigger regeneration* of the damaged surface.
6. The repair is carried out by the host eye's *own cells*.
7. The eye is permanently healed.

This is how Mike received his sight, but the facts of the procedure belie the huge risk involved, as well as the major physiologically and psychologically adjustments Mike had to go through. While the eye is permanently healing, the brain is traumatized and challenged as it attempts to remember how to process visual input. And this, more than the procedure, is the real story of Mike May's journey into eyesight because, ironically, blindness became less challenging and more comfortable to him than sight. The emotional pain was severe too, because his old life, his old way of being, and his old identity as a blind man were becoming a thing of the past. How would this change him? Would his marriage survive? Would sex be the same? What new temptations would sight engender?

Who am I now? he wondered.

Major transitions are uncomfortable, and the new input is challenging. Once new sight is received, there is no turning back or undoing what has been done. A whole new set of risks and unknowns await us.

"I Think I Can Make You See Again"

Jesus called Himself a physician, and He loved to restore sight to the blind.

Sometimes the patients were literally blind, like the man born blind whom Jesus healed physically. Mud made from Jesus's saliva and some nearby dirt took the place of stem cells, but the results were much better. Take a look at the gospel film and discover how "seeing" is believing:

> Jesus heard that they had thrown him out, and when he found him [the man who had been healed of his blindness], he said, "Do you believe in the Son of Man?"
>
> "Who is he, sir?" the man asked. "Tell me so that I may believe in him."
>
> Jesus said, "You have now seen him; in fact, he is the one speaking with you."
>
> Then the man said, "Lord, I believe," and he worshiped him.
>
> Jesus said, "For judgment I have come into this world, so that the blind will see and those who see will become blind."
>
> Some Pharisees who were with him heard him say this and asked, "What? Are we blind too?"
>
> Jesus said, "If you were blind, you would not be guilty of sin; but now that you claim you can see, your guilt remains. (John 9:35–41)

For Jesus, the end game of the whole episode was not physical healing but spiritual insight. Jesus healed the man so that in the end he could see Jesus and be spiritually healed through *the revelation of God* before him: "You have now seen him; in fact, he is the one speaking with you" (verse 37).

But the whole purpose of revelation is integration and application, as in, "Do you believe in the Son of Man?" (verse 35). Without a decision regarding the new revelation of God, the whole encounter really would be a loss for the man. Jesus served Himself up on a silver platter, and the result was salvation: "Then the man said, 'Lord, I believe,' and he worshiped him" (verse 38).

The signs of healing were great, but the intention of the healing was to bring attention to believing and trusting Jesus for ultimate spiritual healing, salvation, and transformation.

Don't miss this: eyesight for Jesus was insight into Himself.

The Pharisees, blinded by their insecurities and pride, were unable to adjust and see the revelation of God. They had become unteachable, and their thinking had turned stale and stagnant. In the process, they lost their sight. Their sin was pride, and their destiny was to forever remain in the dark. The scales would not fall from their eyes, but those humble enough to believe would enter a new world of sight and insight.

> *Don't miss this: eyesight for Jesus was insight into Himself.*

The process of seeing as a believer goes like this:

1. Our perceptions of reality meet God's revelations of reality.
2. God's revelations meet our disposition (humility or pride).
3. Our disposition produces a decision (accept or reject).
4. An integration of revelation (acceptance) leads to connection, salvation, and transformation with God.
5. The rejection of revelation leads to loss of connection, separation, and stagnation with God.

This story of the blind man and the Pharisees, their encounter with Jesus, and their respective destinies is our story. This is also the story of all living believers and their encounter with the Holy Spirit right *now*. There was a moment in time when, like the blind man, revelation was given for salvation. Jesus was revealed. We believed that revelation of His person and work for us on the cross. Now, Jesus says to His disciples that the job of the Holy Spirit is to continue revealing the mind of Christ to the believer on a continuous basis. Burn these words on your brain for a right relationship with the Holy Spirit:

> But when he, the Spirit of truth, comes, he will guide you into all truth. He will not speak on his own; he will speak only what he hears, and he will tell you what is yet to come. *He will bring glory to me by taking from what is mine and making it known to you.* All that belongs to the Father is mine. *That is why I said the Spirit will take from what is mine and make it known to you.* (John 16:13–15)

Jesus does not need to repeat Himself, but with respect to the age between His departure and His return, He was compelled to say it twice in the same breath to His disciples then and now. He is emphatic that they get this one thing: the Holy Spirit is coming to bring truth and to change the way we perceive and process reality by giving us the mind of Christ so that in *all* things we can live out the will of God in *all* ways for *all* of our days on earth. What we need to live right is the mind of Christ, and right thinking produces right living.

It's called discernment.

> The man without the Spirit does not accept the things that come from the Spirit of God, for they are foolishness to him, and he cannot understand them, because they are *spiritually discerned*. *The spiritual man makes judgments about all things,* but he himself is not subject to any man's judgment: "For who has known the mind of the Lord that he may instruct him?" But *we have the mind of Christ*. (1 Corinthians 2:14–16)

More than anything, what Jesus's disciples needed in His absence was His mind on all matters. And it's still the number one need of a disciple.

True wisdom is the domain of God, and His agent for that wisdom is the Holy Spirit.

Three unmistakable truths must be digested. First, the Holy Spirit is the search engine for all things about God. Second, the Holy Spirit lives in you. Third, God reveals His wisdom to believers by the Holy Spirit.

Through the Holy Spirit, a Christian finds himself saying on a continuous basis, "Oh, *now* I see," as spiritual revelations about how life is supposed to work change his perceptions and decision-making filters. You already have God's mind on the matter. All you have to do is Google God through the Holy Spirit.

The process of Googling God on all matters concerning your relationship with Him, your relationships with others, and His will for your life is called *spiritual discernment*. In fact, the Bible declares that we are to Google God's mind and make judgments based on His input "in all things," but a believer still gets to choose the search engines of wisdom that are out there: you can Google self, your culture, or God. That choice and the input that comes back determine the way you think and, in turn, will determine the person you become: "For as he thinks within himself, so he is" (Proverbs 23:7, NASB).

Donor Cells

The Holy Spirit is in you to change the way you think about everything. He is lending you His donor cells of thought straight from Jesus, laying them over your own diseased thinking, and triggering the regeneration of new insight that promotes spiritual eyesight. These new thoughts eventually fuse with your thoughts to build a new intuition. The continuous and ongoing repair of our thinking is carried out over time by our own willing cooperation. The results are freedom and healing, or as the Bible describes the process, "to be *made new in the*

> **soar fact**
> *The Holy Spirit is in you to change the way you think about everything.*

attitude of your minds; and to put on the new self, created to be like God in true righteousness and holiness" (Ephesians 4:23–24).

You can recognize the Holy Spirit's work in your thinking in five very specific ways that reflect these new attitudes.

1. The Holy Spirit changes my interpretations of negative situations to bring clarity.

> *Consider it* pure joy, my brothers, whenever you face trials of many kinds, because you know that the testing of your faith develops perseverance. Perseverance must finish its work *so that you may be mature and complete,* not lacking anything. (James 1:2–4)

Translation: The Holy Spirit changes the way we see and filter our circumstances. Only through the Holy Spirit can obstacles become divine opportunities. Only through the Holy Spirit can stumbling blocks be changed into steppingstones toward maturity and personal growth. Only through the Holy Spirit can God take a sin that Satan intended to destroy us with and use it to develop us into the men who gain victory over it. The Holy Spirit's job in your life is to redeem your mind by reframing your circumstances through the filter of God's purposes. He delivers to your mind and heart the assurance that "God *causes all things to work together* for good to those who love God, to those who are called according to His purpose," (Romans 8:28, NASB). The result: you rise above your circumstances.

> *Only through the Holy Spirit can obstacles become divine opportunities.*

2. The Holy Spirit reshapes the impressions of my emotions in order to bring reality.

> I say to God my Rock, "Why have you forgotten me? Why must I go about mourning, oppressed by the enemy?" My bones suffer mortal agony as my foes

taunt me, saying to me all day long, "Where is your God?" Why are you down-cast, O my soul? Why so disturbed within me? *Put your hope in God, for I will yet praise him, my Savior and my God."* (Psalm 42:9–11)

Translation: The job of the Holy Spirit is to remind us that when there is a loving God on our side, nothing is ever fatal or final. Emotions are powerful, and God knows that, left unchecked, they can take over our whole existence. He also knows that Satan loves to exploit out-of-control emotions with lies that lead us to do self-destructive and harmful things. But the Holy Spirit is not just there for the lows and bad times. He is also there to temper our successes so that we don't hit the slippery slope of pride and self-sufficiency.

> *The job of the Holy Spirit is to remind us that when there is a loving God on our side, nothing is ever fatal or final.*

3. The Holy Spirit simplifies my convictions, which produce actions that bring the highest possible spiritual integrity.

Jesus replied: " 'Love the Lord your God with all your heart and with all your soul and with all your mind.' This is the first and greatest commandment. And the second is like it: 'Love your neighbor as yourself.' All the Law and the Prophets hang on these two commandments." (Matthew 22:37–40)

Translation: The Holy Spirit will always reveal the mind of Christ in decision making and move us in the simple direction of doing that one thing that shows love for God and love for people. The Holy Spirit's fingerprints are synonymous with spiritual simplicity, which leads to clarity and integrity.

4. The Holy Spirit reminds me of my identity, which creates inner security.

For you did not receive a spirit that makes you a slave again to fear, but you received the Spirit of sonship. And by him we cry, "Abba, Father." The Spirit himself testifies with our spirit that we are God's children. (Romans 8:15–16)

Translation: The Holy Spirit changes the way we think about ourselves to create a secure and accepted man who seeks to please God. Versus what? An insecure man who battles for the acceptance of others, who seeks to please people, and who loses his identity in the process. The Holy Spirit tells us over and over, "Your Dad loves you." And as we let in the truth about how God feels about us, we transform and become "more than conquerors through him who loved us" (Romans 8:37).

5. The Holy Spirit reminds me of my future, which gives me confidence in the present.

For those God foreknew he also predestined to be conformed to the likeness of his Son, that he might be the firstborn among many brothers. And those he predestined, he also called; those he called, he also justified; those he justified, he also glorified." (Romans 8:29–30)

Translation: When a man feels good about the vision he is working toward, he confidently pursues it. The Holy Spirit reminds every believer that a very specific process of becoming like Christ (see my book *Dream*) and a very specific plan for the future will be executed because we are *in Christ*. I call it the end zone dance. It is a moment in time when we celebrate the victory of Christ and our own part in that victory. The end zone is in sight, as is the glory that goes with it.

Activity *with* Insight

When the Holy Spirit enlightens a man, He explains things and makes clear the will of God. His personality and mission are intimately linked to affecting our thinking, and in doing so, He influences our living. His knowledge, power, authority, and proximity to God's Man gives the Holy Spirit the swing vote on all matters of life. The more we allow Him to be the primary shaper of our thoughts, the more He will act upon, affect, inspire, and change our life.

The Holy Spirit heals ignorance, prejudice, immaturity, and superstition, and He replaces them with a sound understanding of the facts from God's perspective.

The best use of Holy Spirit power in your life—the same power that raised Christ from the dead and put Him over all things—is to give you a new set of eyes.

In chapter 6 we learned that His job is to influence our thinking through *warning* that leads to life and peace. In this chapter we learned how He influences through *insight* that leads to new ways to process and perceive reality. Both are manifestations of His transforming power. But this totally new way of perceiving reality is a battle of the mind. There are competing identities, voices, and impulses all at war to win over how we think about and perceive reality.

> *The Holy Spirit heals ignorance, prejudice, immaturity, and superstition, and He replaces them with a sound understanding of the facts from God's perspective.*

In ways similar to what Mike May experienced on his journey to sight, our transitions on the way to embracing the Holy Spirit's role in our life are uncomfortable and challenging. Once we receive new eyes through salvation and new revelation, there is no turning back or undoing the implantation. The work of mental transformation is under way.

By saying yes to eyesight from the Holy Spirit, we have bitten off whole new sets of risks and unknowns, which will change forever the way we live. The only question is this: What response will we have to all of this? Will ours be the humble acceptance of the blind man or the prideful rejection of the Pharisee?

Let's pray together:

> *Holy Spirit, like the blind man healed by Jesus, I want the works of God displayed in my life. I want my thoughts to be examined and the way I perceive things to be given new life. I want the scarred tissues of my mind, which keep me from seeing things the way You see them, healed. I want spiritual eyesight through Your insight.*
>
> *Enlighten the eyes of my heart, Holy Spirit, by revealing the mind of Christ to me on all things, especially those ways of thinking that hold me captive to fear instead of obedient to faith. Help me to make solid and sound decisions based on*

Your counsel. Help me to see my relationships with God and
people through the filter of Your promises and commands.

I reject other voices in my life that pollute Your
counsel and inspire sin. I submit to Your loving author-
ity and friendly voice in the midst of my life. Lord,
Holy Spirit, I believe and worship You. I am hungry for
Your wisdom and Your Word. And I am listening, in
Jesus's name. Amen.

all is yours

You cannot antagonize and influence at the same time.

—JOHN KNOX

I am not a free-will hugger by nature.

My pastor, on the other hand, is "huggy bear" and proud of it.

I am privileged to see the love machine in action on a daily basis around Saddleback Church, greeting and squeezing first-time visitors on the patio, vice-gripping fellow pastors back in the greenroom before he goes to the pulpit, and publicly cuddling up to his staff in the church's hallways. He is the most aggressive and appropriate giver of affection on the planet. But here's the deal: it's not just with people he knows around the church, it's with *everybody*. Think out-of-control, tail-wagging, soft, bouncing Labrador puppy, and you are getting close.

At Every Man Ministries we host trainings called Intentional Men's Ministry. A class of ten to fifteen pastors gathers for two days of focused sessions, fellowship, and personal growth. Every time I host these pastors, I am just waiting for you-know-who to burst through the door and start loving on all our attendees. No one knows the day or hour; all you know is that it is going to happen if he is in town. It's like having the Daily Double hiding underneath the board on *Jeopardy*. All of a sudden, a regular moment in the day gets turned over and in he comes, grinning, hugging, taking pictures, sitting down to talk, and cracking jokes.

It reminds me of the dramatic Kramer entrances that were a hallmark of *Seinfeld*: dramatic, goofy, unexpected, and above all, welcomed.

His first words are always the same: "Hey, everybody!" Based on the volume level, you'd swear he was six or seven years old.

Every one in the room is smiling, because they are in the presence of full acceptance from a man who they know carries a ton of influence around the world.

That is my pastor, Rick Warren, a man who knows how to love on people. Oh, and every time he leaves our conversations, he never fails to say, "I love you, Kenny." I know what you are thinking: *Are you kidding me?* In the middle of what has to be one of the craziest lives on the planet, you get Rick's presence, love, and hugs.

Outsiders are disappointed if they are looking for juicy gossip, because the man is consistent. It's not an act. Ask his wife. Ask his staff. Ask the visitor to Saddleback who bumps into him on the patio. He is the same dude in public and private settings, on Sunday and Wednesday, preaching to tens of thousands or personally hugging a visiting Korean delegation. He is a free man.

When I step back and look at my pastor, I see the deep works of the Holy Spirit in him. I trust you, like me, are after deeper works of the Holy Spirit in the areas of your life that matter most to *Him*. That's my pastor's heart, and that's my heart too.

So over the next four chapters we will look at the main transformations of character the Holy Spirit wants to address in the life of every believer. These four areas are His deepest, most profound, and life-altering works that bring freedom, healing, and influence to the cooperating follower of Jesus. They also are the four areas where Satan contends most vigorously for control—no big surprise there (see my book *Fight*). He hates a free, healed, Spirit-filled, and Spirit-fruit-producing believer wreaking havoc upon his evil plans for a desperate world. It's a control thing with him. Why do I mention this? Because, as you interact with the content of the next four chapters, you, too, will feel Satan coming after you and looking for a fight.

The Deepest Work

Feelings deep within us rise up when it comes to a very personal and powerful issue like how you and I love others, because the first area of freedom and healing the Holy Spirit wants to accomplish in our character concerns our ability to love. By that I mean our personal ability to connect with, accept, serve, encourage, and resolve conflict with others *the way the Holy Spirit wants us to.* That makes all men squirm a little.

Rick Warren has helped me enormously on this topic. First, he is a strong man with aggressive convictions, tons of vision and knowledge, and off-the-chart skills. But get this: *he is really easy to be around.* That quality stands out. Second, Rick is secure in who he is. He does not play to people, and he is free to engage everybody he meets. That quality stands out too. Third (and I can say this based on knowing him as friend and pastor for almost twenty years), he chooses not to retaliate when attacked by Christians and non-

> *Feelings deep within us rise up when it comes to a very personal and powerful issue like how you and I love others, because the first area of freedom and healing the Holy Spirit wants to accomplish in our character concerns our ability to love.*

Christians alike. He loves his enemies by refusing to get angry and attack back. That really stands out, especially when there are tens of thousands in his own congregation who would like to take a whack at the critics, because Rick Warren was the one who introduced them to Christ. But he won't let them do it. He won't let *me* do it! Only a secure and free man in the Spirit can take such a posture. Here's what the apostle Paul had to say about such qualities:

> You, my brothers, were *called to be free.* But do not use your freedom to indulge the sinful nature; rather, *serve one another in love.* The entire law is summed up

in a single command: "*Love your neighbor as yourself.*" If you keep on biting and devouring each other, watch out or you will be destroyed by each other.

So I say, live by the Spirit, and you will not gratify the desires of the sinful nature. (Galatians 5:13–16)

My fangs come out in relationships more than I'd like, and to my shame, I have retaliated against some of my critics instead of prayed for them. I struggle with loving as Paul describes. But I want a deeper work of the Holy Spirit in my relationships, and I believe the Holy Spirit is knocking on that door labeled "Loving Others," inviting me in for a breakthrough. He wants me free. He wants my fangs filed down. He wants my tail wagging. He wants me to subdue the dark impulse for retaliation. He wants me connecting, not compet-ing. He wants me to lift others up, not drag them through the mud. He wants kindness over contention.

> *In all relationships we are leaving somebody either a little better or a little worse.*

There is no such thing as neutral in human relationships. There is no such thing as "nobody else is getting hurt" or "nobody else needs to know." In all relationships we are leaving somebody either a little better or a little worse. The Holy Spirit's mission in your life is to enlarge versus diminish your relationships by delivering you from self-absorption and helping you become free in Christ's love so that you can love oth-ers better.

Unshackled Man

I want to tell a story about a man who, to his surprise, found freedom.

It starts behind bars.

Prison had turned Billy Wilson into a shadow of his former self. For years he deterio-rated in solitary confinement. He was so much more than what he had become, but this place, this cell, had deeply imprinted his identity. He was as hard as the concrete walls he stared at all day long. He had not known freedom for years, and his mind, body, and spirit had fought to stay alive and remain sane.

On a day like any other, his lonely malaise was interrupted by the distant sounds of large steel doors opening. He was surprised, because dinner normally came at 5:00 p.m. on the dot, and it was only three o'clock. The sounds became louder, which meant someone was moving closer.

The big door closest to his cell crashed open. Loud steps beat on the concrete floor. One set of shoes was definitely a guard, but the second was unfamiliar to Billy. Keys clanked and adrenaline invaded his system as he saw the shadows of four feet at his door. A large key slid into the lock, and with one hard twist and pull, his cell door swung open. The light nearly blinded him, but Billy clearly heard the words coming from a face he could hardly see: "Your sentence has been overturned. You're a free man."

The voice belonged to Warden Simpson. Those unfamiliar shoes were his also.

Just like that, everything had changed. Billy knew he should feel elated, but the unknowns outside the prison walls terrified him.

Living and acting free take time.

Billy was processed and released that same day. He was free legally and physically, but the process of making the transition from being Billy the prisoner to Billy the free man would take many years and experiences, as well as a lot of support and counseling. Escaping his former identity and his attachments to his former life were the hardest parts. He had known *only one way* to be for a long time.

Ironically, many of the new opportunities of his freedom were intimidating. And while he wanted to pursue them, the old voices, tapes, faces, and ways of thinking seemed to prevent him from becoming someone different or taking new risks. All the what-ifs, the labels, and the self-doubt beat a hasty retreat back inside the walls of his own mind. Then his inner voice would say, *At least in prison I knew who I was.* It's bizarre, but Billy felt more insecure in his freedom and more secure when he thought about being back in prison.

Sanford, the counselor from the prisoner transition department, met with Billy for coffee every week. He kept encouraging him to embrace new opportunities. Eventually Billy took a job at a manufacturing plant, made some new friends on the company softball team, and even started going to a church men's group that was studying spiritual freedom. Slow but sure, the old voices lost out to Sanford's steady prodding and the fresh experiences validating Billy's new path. It took some time to sink in, but the reality of freedom meant becoming responsible to risk new choices.

Billy still feels funny when others tell him, "You're such a different person." He laughs and smiles a lot more these days. That huge grin of his says that he is finally free *to be free.*

———

All of us who have been set free by Jesus are somewhat like Billy. We are all in that process of learning what it means to *think* like a free man so that we can finally *act* like a free man. The Holy Spirit (the Counselor) was given to us to encourage that process, so we can make the big leap and follow His voice into new freedom. From the first century until now, believers have made the transition from being made free by God, to being set free with new attitudes toward self and God, into finally living free. Here's how the apostle Paul encouraged some first-century Roman Billy Wilsons through the process of learning to walk in their new freedom in Christ:

> So *now* there is no condemnation for those *who belong to Christ Jesus.* And because you belong to him, *the power of the life-giving Spirit has freed you from the power of sin that leads to death.* The law of Moses was unable to save us because of the weakness of our sinful nature. So God did what the law could not do. He sent his own Son in a body like the bodies we sinners have. And in that body *God declared an end to sin's control over us by giving his Son as a sacrifice for our sins.* He did this so that the just requirement of the law would be fully satisfied for us, *who no longer follow our sinful nature but instead follow the Spirit.* (Romans 8:1–4, NLT)

Here's the sad thing: many believers are free but still not walking in that freedom and not experiencing real change. They are free, but they don't think free. The old nature, the old voices, and the old ways of seeing themselves seem safer and still hold sway. They have the Holy Spirit, but they compartmentalize Him away from the real change He seeks to make in their life. They are free people, but they act like they are still prisoners, confined by the walls of their bad thinking about God and themselves.

So what does the Holy Spirit want to say to that person stuck in a prison of his own making?

You don't have to be that person anymore.

Yes, indeed!

Secure Means Free to Love

So what's a common theme in Pastor Rick's behavior, Billy Wilson's story, and greater Holy Spirit freedom in our life and our relationships? One word: *security.*

To risk in any relationship, there must be a sense of security in someone or something that holds us steady in case we are rejected, betrayed, hurt, or abandoned. Jesus was free to love because He was secure in His relationship with His Father. It was the well of security He drew upon to aggressively love people all the way to the cross. So secure was His connection that Jesus regularly did the following:

- He broke the rules of culture to love.
- He sacrificed His own comfort to love.
- He was not intimidated by opinion polls when choosing to love.
- He loved the morally unacceptable.
- He upset religious leaders to love.
- He loved the ethnically unacceptable.
- He loved the physically unacceptable.
- He loved the culturally unacceptable.

Jesus knew without reservation whose He was and that He was headed back to that relationship. It made Him unstoppable.

The Holy Spirit can do the same thing for us…if we let Him. He makes any God's Man more secure in his relationship with God so that he can be free to love the people God has placed in his life. The Holy Spirit is all about closing the gaps between people. Believe me, He's in a boxing match for our relationships. Not just the relationship between us and our wife or girlfriend, our kids, or our friends, but the relationship between us and *everybody.*

> *Jesus knew without reservation whose He was and that He was headed back to that relationship. It made Him unstoppable.*

Let's go ringside and listen to the apostle Paul's bellowing introduction concerning the two contenders fighting for control of our connections with people:

> The *sinful nature* wants to do evil, which is just the opposite of what the *Spirit wants.* And *the Spirit gives us desires* that are the opposite of what the sinful nature desires. *These two forces are constantly fighting each other,* so you are not free to carry out your good intentions. (Galatians 5:17, NLT)

In one corner in my life is self-protection and self-interest, also known as the sinful nature. This is the old, insecure version of me that is worried about my needs being met, while at the same time forgetting that God has already met all my needs. This guy likes to make distinctions, keep tabs, find faults, and whine. When Team Self (protection and interest) has control, my relationships are plagued with mental and emotional garbage, joyless grabs for control, an inability to love or be loved, dividedness, small-mindedness, seeing everyone as a rival, withdrawal, competition for control, unplease-ability, flaring tempers, low blows, apathy, eighth-grade threats, unmet needs, loneliness, separation, and weird, hurtful solutions about how I can feel better about all the pain I have caused others.

Simply put, I am miserable, and people suffer when the old self is calling the shots. He's a boy not a man, forty-five going on fourteen, immature and feeling unloved, so he's determined to protect himself in order to get what's his.

No bueno.

In the other corner is the reigning champion of all that is healthy and productive in my relationships. When the Holy Spirit dominates my thinking, He frees me to take risks for God with other people and to walk away from the goober I just described. My relationships are blessed with new affection for others, more peace, a new willingness to stick with my commitments, compassion, concern for people I don't even know, less need for me to have my way, real love and loyalty, more public and private displays of affection, less stress, new relationships, a new openness to learn from others, and less regret. It's a wonderful groove, and it's where I want to stay. I feel like a grownup, all of forty-four years old, mature, and much less selfish. My wife, my kids, and all who come in contact with me like this guy much better.

> *When the Holy Spirit dominates my thinking, He frees me to take risks for God with other people.*

Holy Spirit control *es muy bueno*!

Perspective Is Powerful

The trick is how to hold on to this pattern and stoke the fire of the Holy Spirit's work in our relationships. Here are the core insights and interactions the Holy Spirit uses to make all believers feel more secure, able to think outside their own needs, and free to enter into the lives and needs of others. All five perspectives from the Holy Spirit help us love better.

1. The Holy Spirit covers us with a sense of security.

> So then, no more boasting about men! *All things are yours,* whether Paul or Apollos or Cephas or the world or life or death or the present or the future—*all are yours,* and *you are of Christ,* and *Christ is of God.*" (1 Corinthians 3:21–23)

The Holy Spirit reminds us that every believer is a *possessor of everything* in Christ. The man who has God for his portion lacks nothing and has everything that can make him happy. It doesn't matter what church we attend, how much money we make, if we live or die, or who's in the White House. In Christ we possess eternity, mercy, grace, citizenship in heaven, sonship, and total acceptance. This reality frees us to love the people in our life more aggressively and sacrificially. "Remember," He says, "all is yours."

2. The Holy Spirit covers us with a sense of humility.

> For *by the grace given me* I say to every one of you: *Do not think of yourself more highly than you ought,* but rather think of yourself with sober judgment, in accordance with the measure of faith God has given you…. Live in harmony with one another. *Do not be proud,* but be willing to associate with people of low position. *Do not be conceited.* (Romans 12:3, 16)

The Holy Spirit reminds us of the full measure of acceptance and affirmation God has given us to enter into relationship with Him. It grieves the Holy Spirit when we willfully take all of God's grace, but we're greedy with His grace in our relationships. It is a sobering thought and puts us in the right frame of mind to connect with others, forgive others, make allowances for others' faults, and pursue peace with others. "Remember," He says, "but for the grace of God in your life, where would you be?"

3. The Holy Spirit covers us with a sense of camaraderie.

> Just as each of us has one body with many members, and these members do not all have the same function, so in Christ we who are many form one body, and *each member belongs to all the others.*" (Romans 12:4–5)

The Holy Spirit likes to say, "That's your brother" and "That's your sister." As a dad and a son, I know how this works. God is big on His children being each other's biggest fans, biggest helps, and biggest supporters—not their biggest critics. He also likes to remind us that, by design, our brothers and sisters in Christ are not like us! We need everybody's unique skills to get the kingdom job done. Since I am big on sports and execution on the field or on the court, I get this, and it makes me love my spiritual family more. Beginning with my wife, Chrissy, my kids, my friends, my small group, and my church family locally and globally, my mission is to encourage and appreciate how God has gifted them. As a result, the body of Christ is more unified. "Remember," He says, "you are all on the same team!"

4. The Holy Spirit covers us with a deep sense of accountability.

> For none of us lives to himself alone and none of us dies to himself alone. *If we live, we live to the Lord; and if we die, we die to the Lord. So, whether we live or die, we belong to the Lord.* For this very reason, Christ died and returned to life so that he might be the Lord of both the dead and the living. You, then, why do you judge your brother? Or why do you look down on your brother? For we will all stand before God's judgment seat. It is written: "'As surely as I live,' says the Lord, 'every knee will bow before me; every tongue will confess to God.'" So then, *each of us will give an account of himself to God.* (Romans 14:7–12)

This is one of the most freeing and powerful reminders the Holy Spirit gives to believers about their relationships. A day is approaching for every one of us when we'll meet God face to face and give an account. In the end, His approval and opinion are the only things that will matter that day. This means that God's Man can love, connect, and change aggressively to make his relationships healthy, because he lives for an audience of one. This was Jesus's approach while on earth: fearless before men as He sacrificially loved people and pleased the Father to whom He was returning. "Remember," He says, "you exist to please God alone, so live for an audience of one."

5. The Holy Spirit covers us with a sense of urgency.

> Love does no harm to its neighbor. Therefore love is the fulfillment of the law. And do this, understanding the present time. The hour has come for you to wake up from your slumber, because our salvation is nearer now than when we first believed. The night is nearly over; the day is almost here. So let us put aside the deeds of darkness and put on the armor of light. (Romans 13:10–12)

The Holy Spirit reminds us that our highest priority on earth is time sensitive. The clock is winding down every day. This reality invests every interaction, encounter, and relationship with greater meaning. Knowing this frees us to love like never before, with focus and attention, the people God brings into our life. We don't delay as much in offering forgiveness, we say "I am sorry" faster, we risk more to connect with strangers, we minister with more care, and we teach with more urgency. "Remember," He says, "you're it, and time is short!"

When it comes to loving others, the Bible does not reveal an emotional love like we see in the movies or read about in novels. Biblical love usually speaks to the will. Jesus said, "My command is this: Love each other as I have loved you" (John 15:12). To that end the gospels show a Savior sweating blood in a garden and going against His emotions and

> *The Holy Spirit reminds us that our highest priority on earth is time sensitive.*

discomfort to love *sacrificially*. The ones on the receiving end of this love experience a deep gratitude because sacrificial love stirs up deep emotions. This is you and me. We have experienced and felt this amazing love of God through the Holy Spirit's presence and work in our lives, so in response, suddenly we pick up our cross, make our sacrifice, and die our own deaths to self.

All is ours!

> *Holy Spirit, I hand over all of my relationships to You. I want all of Your love and peace to come. I want all of Your gentleness and kindness to come through me to the people in my life. Help me to find my security in my relationship and destiny with the Father, as Jesus did.*
>
> *Cover me, Holy Spirit, with a newfound spirit of humility before people, a spirit of camaraderie with other believers, a spirit of security as a possessor of all things meaningful in Christ, a spirit of accountability as I live for an audience of one, and a spirit of urgency as I recognize there is only a short time on earth for me to love my neighbor as myself. Help me to think free and act freely in Christ. Amen.*

deeply satisfied

The discontented are never rich; the contented never poor.

—George Eliot

"Kenny, I am at the hospital. Haley is in the intensive care unit and…"

The father on the other end of the call was my friend Rob. His horrifying words were coming through an earpiece while Chrissy and I drove our daughter Cara and her date to the school prom. His words crashed into my brain like an eighteen-wheeler, bending and twisting my thoughts and emotions beyond comprehension. I hope I never have to hear such words again.

Rob was being crushed by hopelessness as his child's life was ebbing away before his eyes. All her vital signs were headed in the wrong direction. It was immobilizing for me as a father, looking at my daughter, who was all dolled up and stunning in her prom dress. Time slowed. I was lost in my own numbness until Rob's request audibly punctured my malaise.

"Can you come to the hospital?"

"We are praying right now for Haley," I replied. "Chrissy and I will be right over."

I clicked off the earpiece and took a quick read of the faces in the car, which all said, *Well? What's going on?*

Cara was the first to ask, "Dad, what's wrong?"

I looked into the eyes of my own shining, beautiful seventeen-year-old (the same age as Haley), so full of hope and life, and gave it to her straight: "My friend's daughter is in the intensive care unit at Mission Hospital, and it's not looking good. We need to pray *right now.*" All of us did just that until we arrived at the school. After dropping off Cara and her date, Chrissy and I proceeded to enter the worst hell a parent can ever see.

The intensive care unit doors swung open, and we saw a surreal scene of nurses on phones, crying friends with hands clasped over their chests, and just beyond them, a room that was full of emergency medical specialists and nurses working on Haley. Rob and his wife, Deborah, were watching helplessly. I walked past the nurses' desk into their living nightmare. Their beautiful girl lay lifeless on the gurney, intubated, pupils dilated, and nonresponsive, with six IVs puncturing her smooth, dark skin. No words, a quick hug for my friend, and I turned to face, touch, and ask Jesus to speak life into this young body.

I never doubted her healing—immediate or ultimate—but as a father of a child her exact age and almost exact appearance, I bit down hard on this one, praying urgently, fervently, and earnestly for four hours. It was a roller-coaster ride dictated by flashing green numbers on monitors to tell us if our efforts were succeeding. On three separate occasions her heart had to be restarted through chest compressions.

Finally, at eleven thirty that night, the physician called the family into a small consult room and gave the "speech." Medically, there was nothing left to do. Haley was gone neurologically, and all her systems had shut down. It was over. I walked my friend Rob and his family into Haley's room and watched as they said their good-byes to their daughter and sister. Rob and Deborah's little girl, nicknamed Teaspoon, was gone, and for them, the nightmare was just beginning.

The Burning Bush

Six days later I stood with the family again in the greenroom of our church for the next hardest moment of this ordeal. Over a thousand students, friends, neighbors, and family had gathered for Haley's memorial service. The most emotionally demanding message I have ever had to give started like this:

> Jesus said, "I am the resurrection and the life. He who believes in Me will live, even though he dies; and whoever lives and believes in Me will never die."
>
> Today's memorial service will no doubt be bittersweet. Bitter because everyone is saddened and shocked at Haley's passing. Sad because so many didn't have a chance to say good-bye. But there is also the sweet because of the tender memories that have been pouring out for a daughter, a granddaughter, a sister, a friend, a cousin, a fellow student, jokester, employee, and helping soul.

Looking at Rob and Deborah and choking back tears, I labored on with my opening remarks:

> Rob and Deborah… There is absolutely no way in a service or in a day or in a lifetime that we can properly pay tribute to your precious daughter and comfort your family. Words are so one-dimensional, and Haley's life was so full and complex. But we can do our best to do three things today. And if we can just do these three things, that will be enough for now.
>
> Rob and Deborah… Our first priority is to comfort you and your family. Our second responsibility is to honor and remember your daughter and her place in our lives. And lastly we want to stand with you and look forward to the future…taking some small baby steps together.

Then, lifting my eyes from our semiprivate conversation, I raised my head to the thousand plus assembled in the worship center and addressed them as I would like to address you right now:

> For the rest of us present, the Bible says it is good for us to be here today… "It is better to go to a house of mourning than to a house of feasting." The writer

of Ecclesiastes said, "For death is the destiny of every man; the living should take this to heart. Sorrow is better than laughter, because a sad face is good for the heart. The heart of the wise is in the house of mourning, but the heart of fools is in the house of pleasure" [Ecclesiastes 7:2–4].

The Bible says that days like today act like Windex, clearing away the unessential and peripheral, and clarifying for us what we should really be focusing on and how we should be living. Haley's final gift to all of us is a chance to think about the time we have left and how we will now invest it as all of us prepare for eternity. Will you pray with me and commit yourself and this service to God?

After concluding that prayer, I looked into the eyes of those people before me. The room was completely motionless. Every countenance was present and glued to my face, quiet and ready to listen to my voice speaking on behalf of God. It was unreal, as though each person had become emotionally homeless, had been given a bowl, and was standing patiently in line for a meal at God's rescue mission. The Holy Spirit was standing over the large, steaming pot of God's truth, and I was the ladle in His hand that would portion out to each individual a personal word from the Lord.

All pride was gone. All superficiality vaporized. All complaint vanquished. All petty concerns incinerated. All self-absorption defeated. All divisions set aside. All coveting and comparing were gone. All that remained before me was brokenness and openness. Everyone present stood vulnerable and accessible to the Holy Spirit for a life inspection and personal revelation.

What did He say in those next moments? Three very specific things He also wants to say to us right now:

- Quit looking for contentment in the wrong places.
- Be grateful for the blessings of God you still possess.
- Get crackin' on your relationships with God and people while there is still time.

After Haley's service, reports of burning-bush encounters with the Holy Spirit started flooding in. The most authentic report of an encounter with the Holy Spirit came from a man who relayed what happened in his own way: "Everybody's BS left the room." His words, not mine.

When I asked him what he meant, he said, "Are you kidding me? After this, I am driving straight home to my wife and daughter, hugging them, kissing them, and thanking God!"

The words from Ecclesiastes proved a prophetic harbinger of the reality that slammed into people's spirits. Solomon's observation about the house of mourning being a place of transformation came alive right in front of my eyes. Sorrow and pain were the teachers, the Holy Spirit was counseling everyone, and "the living" were taking the lesson to heart. He gave us all God's glasses as we entered into the pain of Haley's passing and made us look from God's perspective at our life. And from this angle came powerful insight into what's wrong in us, what blessings we have taken for granted, and what our responsibility is to God and people on earth.

The wise take moments such as these to heart.

A Broken Spirit

A broken spirit is what makes room for the Holy Spirit's powerful presence and ministry in our lives. In fact, when God sees that we have been humbled by a circumstance or situation, He gets excited about how that can be used to create humility and a new door for meaningful worship. Listen to David describe the connection: "You do not delight in sacrifice, or I would bring it; you do not take pleasure in burnt offerings. The sacrifices of God are a broken spirit; a broken and contrite heart, O God, you will not despise" (Psalm 51:16–17).

> *A broken spirit is what makes room for the Holy Spirit's powerful presence and ministry in our lives.*

A humbling experience creates new openness; new openness welcomes new revelation of and new intimacy with God; and new intimacy with God breeds awe and wonder over what is transpiring.

Awe is our response to the work of the Holy Spirit in helping us to see and perceive reality. Wonder is the feeling that wells up inside us over the possibilities of a future filled with the blessings of new choices that emanate from this new insight.

As we are learning, this powerful phenomenon of the Holy Spirit is called transcendence, and it works to transform the way we think and live. As we learn to embrace His leadership personally, trust His voice, and move obediently, we find ourselves rising above the obstacles inside and outside of us. Call this what you want, but I call it victory!

The Holy Spirit's first transformational work after salvation is to knead the love of God into every area of our bondage and hurt, creating a new security of soul, after which He explodes that freedom and healing outward and into our connections with others.

The second transformational mission of the Holy Spirit is to liberate us from looking to sources other than God for fulfillment by teaching us to accept, be grateful for, and live contently in the life God has given us, as it is. (Versus what? As it isn't.)

All human beings struggle to reconcile their reality with their expectations. There is the life we thought we would be living, and then there is the life God has purposed and called us to live. One vision and version of life meets our needs for security, comfort, and relief while the other grows our character and our faith. This spiritual battle is worldwide, transcends culture, and is a highly personal process for every believer.

The Holy Spirit encourages believers to trust that God is at work in their present life and to trust that God's purposes for them are being worked out. The dark voices of the flesh and the devil encourage believers to abandon faith in God and to manage reality by embracing alternative realities outside the will of God as solutions. When our character is struggling to meet the demands and pressures our reality is placing upon us, we become vulnerable to the dark voices. That is, easier begins to sound a lot better than working through God's process.

Enter gratitude.

In my retelling of Haley's memorial service, you witnessed the Holy Spirit deliver the knockout punch to one man who couldn't wait to respond to God's revelation. C. S. Lewis wrote about how it feels when the Holy Spirit does this: "The happiest moments are those when we forget our precious selves...but have everything else (God, fellow humans, animals, the garden, and the sky) instead."[3]

By contrast, we know the feelings inside, the attitudes, and the perceptions about our lives when the darker, less mature, and more selfish voices are winning the battle. It's called comparison, jealousy, and envy. Deep inside, our thoughts gravitate powerfully to the "if onlys" that would make our life better. Take your pick:

- If only I had a wife like John's.
- If only I didn't live in this part of the world.
- If only I had a job like his.
- If only I could drive a car like that.
- If only I worked for that company.
- If only people respected me like him.
- If only things were easier for me.
- If only I had a hard body like that dude.
- If only I hadn't screwed up so bad.
- If only I had a normal family situation.
- If only I was pastoring at *that* church.
- If only...

On and on it goes. When we listen to what the dark side is shoveling, we end up feeling and acting unhappy with our life and envious over the advantages, fortunes, or possessions of others. The result? I start becoming blind to the blessings in life. A spirit of ingratitude and complaining soon permeates my existence. The constant comparison kills my contentment. Subconsciously, I become angry at God's providence in my life. My spirit of ingratitude passes the baton on to a spirit of complaining, which runs with the discontent further into the depths of my being. Then my anger leaks out in my being demanding, touchy, and confrontational. Pretty soon I am unpleasant to be around as my attitudes and actions create separation between reason and me, God and me, the people I am closest to and me, and reality and me. The only safe thing left for me to do is to run toward the lies being whispered in my ear.

Satan has a huge stake in my discontentment.

Negative emotions give him the tools he needs to control me. Wherever you find ingratitude, discontent, jealousy, envy, anger, resentment, coveting, constant complaining, and the relational fractures they bring, there's no need to look far for a villain. Just say, "Hi, Satan." He knows that if I am ungrateful in an area of my life, I will have a hard time believing God in that same area. So discontentment is just the opening Satan needs, because I will stay stuck, get frustrated, and be looking for solutions outside of God in that area. Once again it looks like there's a boy in a man's body on the warpath, causing all sorts of damage.

> *Satan has a huge stake in my discontentment.*

In Old Testament times, Israel was notorious for converting "awe and wonder" into "common and forgettable." Observe their destructive pattern recounted by the psalmist:

> In the sight of their fathers he performed wonders
>> in the land of Egypt, in the fields of Zoan.
> He divided the sea and let them pass through it,
>> and made the waters stand like a heap.
> In the daytime he led them with a cloud,
>> and all the night with a fiery light.
> He split rocks in the wilderness
>> and gave them drink abundantly as from the deep.
> He made streams come out of the rock
>> and caused waters to flow down like rivers.
> Yet they sinned still more against him,
>> rebelling against the Most High in the desert.

They tested God in their heart
>   by demanding the food they craved.
They spoke against God, saying,
>   "Can God spread a table in the wilderness?" (Psalm 78:12–19, ESV)

Israel received multiple blessings from God during the Exodus, and yet, as God blessed, His people became more difficult to please, demanding, discontented, and ungrateful. Their example, the apostle Paul told the Corinthians, was given to us as an object lesson on how not to work with God. The key to winning this battle is the same today as it was back then: reflect, remember, and say "thank you" continuously.

> When the LORD your God brings you into the land he swore to your fathers, to Abraham, Isaac and Jacob, to give you—a land with large, flourishing cities you did not build, houses filled with all kinds of good things you did not provide, wells you did not dig, and vineyards and olive groves you did not plant—then when you eat and are satisfied, *be careful that you do not forget the LORD,* who brought you out of Egypt, out of the land of slavery. (Deuteronomy 6:10–12)

God's people walked into a very high standard of living and blessing they did not earn. God gave it all to them. All He asked was that, in their abundance, they would not forget Him or want the lifestyle and customs of the people around them. The one command would help them keep the other.

Unfortunately, they took God's blessings for granted, became hard to please, and set themselves up for the rod to break them of their ingratitude. You see their foolishness over and over, and as a Father, it drove God crazy. (If you are a dad, you know exactly what I am talking about when it comes to ungrateful kids.) The miraculous became mundane. Indifference replaced gratitude. The fear of the Lord and accountability to God were replaced by presumption and entitlement, which resulted in a casual attitude toward God's commands.

In your own life, complaining about stuff and bemoaning your lot may seem harmless, but God takes it very personally. Nothing provokes the anger of the Father more than ingratitude.

The champion of awe and wonder in your life is the Holy Spirit, and when He is dominating this boxing match of the mind, He is causing you to *remember and thankfully recognize God's providence in your life, especially in times of change and challenge.* It's called contentment, joy, peace, and happiness. Deep inside, the Holy Spirit prompts me to see all the things I have versus what I don't have. My thoughts of thanksgiving gravitate toward the blessings of God, beginning with His grace and mercy toward me in Christ.

> *Nothing provokes the anger of the Father more than ingratitude.*

The Holy Spirit says to me, *Pause and take your pick of some of these blessings: your sins have been forgiven, you have a purpose for living, you have a future in heaven, you have the blessings of His Word in your life and how they have been a lamp for your feet, you have been kept from falling into innumerable ditches, you have the blessing of life and breath, you have the blessing of food in your fridge, you have the blessing of a paycheck this week, you have the blessing of being the husband of an amazing woman, you have the blessing of being a dad to your kids, you have the blessing of being able to serve the living God in some small way, you have the blessing of being able to teach His Word and influence people, and you have the blessing of sitting on your back porch on a cool night and staring at the stars.* That's just the tip of the iceberg in my life, just the starters of His miraculous works on my behalf.

For every blessing, a thank-you is in order. And what are the results of saying thank you on a daily basis? *I begin to see even more blessings.* I begin to accept and appreciate my life as it is. I stop comparing and feeling jealous over the life others lead. I start solving the mysteries related to my restlessness. I gain increasing levels of contentment. I am more willing to accept and work with the difficult circumstances that enter my life, versus running or withdrawing. I feel more joy, peace, and satisfaction. I am more free in my worship. I am more welcoming and patient. I am more loving and kind. I am much easier to approach and less judgmental. I am less confrontational. Not surprisingly, my relationships with God and people get a ton better! And once again I feel like a man, a grownup, all of forty-five, mature, and less selfish.

Awesome and wonderful.

A Satisfied Man

The Holy Spirit's constant message to every believer is to find satisfaction in God: "For the kingdom of God is not a matter of eating and drinking, *but of righteousness, peace and joy in the Holy Spirit*" (Romans 14:17). Joy and peace are the by-products of contentment and thanksgiving for the life God has assigned to you. When I daily accept my situation in life, good days and bad, the possibilities of joy and peace become realities. There is no such thing as the joyful and peacefully discontented man. But when I learn how to be content, possess it, and fight to preserve its power in my life, all of the fruits of the Spirit are mine.

One of the highest forms of spiritual warfare is also the simplest: stay grateful and content. Here's how.

Aggressive gratitude: "Therefore, since we are receiving a kingdom that cannot be shaken, *let us be thankful,* and so worship God acceptably with reverence and awe" (Hebrews 12:28). You stay in a place of awe and wonder over God's presence, purpose, and plans unfolding in your life by the discipline of gratitude. Notice the language: be thankful. It doesn't say "do thankful,"

> *One of the highest forms of spiritual warfare is also the simplest: stay grateful and content.*

which tells us that the mission of the Holy Spirit in your life is to develop a spirit of thankfulness as a way to be. This means having an awareness of your indebtedness ("since we are receiving a kingdom that cannot be shaken"), acknowledging that God is good in all He does ("worship God acceptably with reverence and awe"), and affirming His goodness with a life of gratitude ("let us be thankful"). To stay satisfied in God, we have to practice thanking God daily and in all circumstances. And remember, in Christ there is always plenty to be thankful for. If you find yourself struggling to come up with stuff, it is a sure sign that the dark voices of the flesh and the devil are plotting some disobedience options for you. Consider yourself warned!

Aggressive godliness: This is what we call the classic one-two punch that will put ingratitude and comparison on the canvas.

But *godliness with contentment is great gain.* For we brought nothing into the world, and we can take nothing out of it. But if we have food and clothing, we *will be content* with that. People who want to get rich fall into temptation and a trap and into many foolish and harmful desires that plunge men into ruin and destruction. For the love of money is a root of all kinds of evil. Some people, eager for money, have wandered from the faith and pierced themselves with many griefs. But you, man of God, flee from all this, and pursue righteousness, godliness, faith, love, endurance and gentleness. (1 Timothy 6:6–11)

The most lethal blow a man can render discontentment is a strong purpose for living. That is why part of the Holy Spirit's mission in your life is to keep you chasing God's purposes. You can't ask for better instruction. Paul tells Timothy the secret of the one-two punch, warns him not to seek contentment outside of God (in this case, chasing a buck), and then tells him to replace that chase with the one other pursuit consistent with his identity.

Aggressive giving: "In everything I did, I showed you that by this kind of hard work *we must help the weak,* remembering the words the Lord Jesus himself said: 'It is *more blessed to give* than to receive'" (Acts 20:35). Sacrificial giving of time, finances, and skills to help others and further God's purposes in the world breaks the power of materialism and brings us in touch with our brothers and ourselves. Paul was in the habit of not neglecting the poor in particular by taking up collections and *personally delivering them.*

> *The most lethal blow a man can render discontentment is a strong purpose for living.*

This was part of the Holy Spirit's work in his life, of teaching him to be content in all circumstances, because the poor taught him to answer the question: What do I really need?

God has always been a friend of the poor, and there is no such thing as a God's Man who distances himself from brothers in need. "Give generously to him and *do so without a grudging heart;* then because of this the LORD your *God will bless you in all your work* and in everything you put your hand to. There will always be poor people in the land. Therefore I command you to *be openhanded toward your brothers and toward the poor* and needy in your land" (Deuteronomy 15:10–11). The Holy Spirit wants to meet you among the poor, to help you see the face of Jesus, and to provide powerful insight into your true needs as you reach out.

Gratitude. Godliness. Giving.

These are the goals of the Holy Spirit in your life. It doesn't require a tragedy or trauma to possess them—only humility, awe, and wonder over His great love toward you…right now, this moment.

Holy Spirit, forgive me for all the times I grumble and complain over my life. I know it displeases the Father when I try to find satisfaction outside of Him by wishing I had someone else's life instead of the one He's calling me to live.

I need Your reminders every day of the multiplied blessings—big and small— of God in my life, beginning this moment with the breath I have to pray this prayer. Help me to see all my blessings, acknowledge them, and praise God for them on an increasing basis. Open my eyes to the goodness of God in my life, and open my heart to the plan of God in my life today.

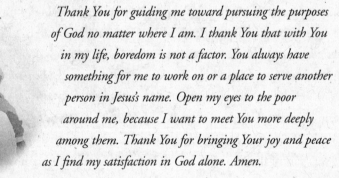

Thank You for guiding me toward pursuing the purposes of God no matter where I am. I thank You that with You in my life, boredom is not a factor. You always have something for me to work on or a place to serve another person in Jesus's name. Open my eyes to the poor around me, because I want to meet You more deeply among them. Thank You for bringing Your joy and peace as I find my satisfaction in God alone. Amen.

done sucking your thumb?

When the fight begins within himself, a man is worth something.
—ROBERT BROWNING

"All right. *That's* it! *You*, come with me!"

Ever hear those words? I have. I heard them from my dad. I heard them from my sixth-grade teacher, Mr. Sievert. And now my son Ryan was hearing those words coming across the kitchen table.

What you'll have to visualize is a preamble of behavior that emotionally amplified my growling edict tenfold. First, imagine the loud noise of a chair being moved irritatingly back from the dinner table as I stood up.

Got it?

Now imagine the simultaneous rapping of my two fists on that same dinner table, initiating the patented "that's enough" stand-up! or the "upright grizzly bear" move. In an instant, a father goes from a subdued posture, head tipped toward his plate, to standing fully erect and dominating the scene with raw size, spit, and growl. It is all instinctive, reactive, and normal fatherly behavior when someone has mistakenly assumed the family rules don't apply to him anymore. A very alpha male display.

Mr. Noisy and Boisterous suddenly became deadly still.

The rest of the family shared the "don't look at Dad right now…Ryan is in deep linguine" look. But the look on their faces was nothing compared to that of the unsuspecting camper now caught within a breath's distance of the menacing grizzly bearing his fangs.

Besides Ryan, not one person at the table was totally shocked. My Academy Award–winning behavior came after a month of Ryan's shenanigans. In fact, I had let things build up on purpose in order to have this little rite-of-passage moment in front of the family with my fourteen-year-old son.

To summarize, let's just say that Ryan had ants in his pants at the dinner table. Normal boy, right? He finishes early, gets bored, forgets his manners, starts bugging his little sister, gets told to quiet down, then presses "Repeat."

I get that. He reminds me of someone I know (ahem) who, for similar reasons at this age, was regularly pulled by his ear down the hall.

In the weeks leading up to the "When Dads Attack" moment, Ryan had elevated his game, you might say. In doing so, the emotional scales had tipped from manageable and tolerable to annoying and disrespectful. That meant more frequent admonitions, interjections, and colorful table discussions.

Chrissy and I had elevated our own game as well to preserve our adult status and to prevent clubbing him. This effort involved reasoning with Ryan about how "taking your time with dinner, eating more slowly, participating in the conversation, being courteous, and not throwing wadded-up napkins in people's drink cups was the behavior *of a man* at the table."

And for the parenting *pièce de résistance,* we even presented Ryan with a scenario about being at a potential in-law's table in the near future and getting a no-confidence vote based on his poor table manners.

All this is to say that the "manners amendment" to Ryan's personal constitution was frequently discussed at the table in the weeks leading up to this manhood moment. All present new exactly why he was getting hauled to the slammer.

Closing the door to his room behind me, I turned and faced my son, who was sitting on the bed, knowing that the next words out of my mouth had to be sincere, firm, and challenging. So I took one of those long, deep breaths, exhaled loudly, and bit down hard enough to leave a mark.

"We're done acting like a boy at the dinner table. I love you, son, but you have got to decide for yourself if you want to stay a boy or become a man who knows how to control himself around other people and show respect. It ends here."

Ryan nodded.

"Now, I have been waiting to see if you would take me at my word, watching, giving you several chances to turn it around. But I see by your behavior that you don't respect me enough to simply take me at my word. So now I have to speak to you not as a coach or a man, which is what I want, but I have to speak to you from the position of an angry father in charge who loves his son enough to yank him aside and deliver some discipline. How does this feel to you?"

> *The hardest victory is victory over self.*

"Not good," he leaked.

"It doesn't feel good to me either. Do you want me to talk to you like the father of a six-year-old who needs some reminding of who's in charge? Or do you want me to talk to you like a coach—we partner together, and you listen so you can be a great man?"

"A coach and partner."

Option A was never really an option.

"Okay, look at me," I said, lowering my energy verbally and physically. I stepped up to him, cupped his red face in my hands, tears now forming in his eyes, looked him in the eye, pulled him to my chest, and kept talking. "You are a Christian, and you are a Luck. God put you in this family for a reason, and one of them is for you to learn what it means to be God's Man. This is what men do who love each other. We care enough to step into each other's face and speak truth when someone's acting like a boy and needs to act like a man. You have my permission to do that with me if I am out of line. Do I have your permission?"

"Yes, Dad."

"Okay, we are going to go back into the kitchen, and you and I are going to do the dishes together. Let's go."

Ryan can count on one hand the number of times I have raised my energy level that way with him. He loves me more than I deserve, and we are becoming the best of friends as he enters the Man Zone. But it was time: time for Ryan to realize that a fight must begin in himself to gain control over his behavior, time to begin taking responsibility for that aspect of his growth, time to learn that sometimes borrowing trouble is not better than avoiding it altogether, and time for Ryan to begin winning some victories over Ryan!

Aristotle once said, "I count him braver who overcomes his desires than him who conquers his enemies; the hardest victory is victory over self."

Yes, my wise Greek brother, very hard!

Borrowing Trouble

Boys borrow trouble.

That is Ryan's passage right now. It is also a stage in our own spiritual maturity that the Holy Spirit wants to successfully guide us through before we damage ourselves and our relationships with God and with people. As a men's pastor to seven thousand men connected in groups, believe me when I say that age (chronological) or achievement has zilch to do with emotional or spiritual maturity. Every week there is a new phone call, new e-mail, or new situation I am brought into that involves a man acting like a teenager with respect to issues that require an adult-size maturity. These men are successful in so many other ways, except the most important ways. Just think about Tiger Woods.

Why would a guy with a high IQ, big money, the right life accessories, and even strong spiritual motivation become secretly captive to a behavior or way of thinking to the point of losing all external successes in order to keep a destructive habit?

Having walked so many dudes through the healing process, I find the root of the struggle is typically an unhealed aspect of their manhood: a hurt, a wound, a failure, a deep need to have control over something, a missing relationship, a trauma from the past, or a source of shame that handicaps their ability to whip certain behaviors. In other words, for whatever reason, the boy stopped growing into a man emotionally, relationally, spiritually, or all three combined. As a consequence, the man acts like a boy on a particular issue, unable to control his behavior or change, justifying his actions, and borrowing trouble. The older men get, the sillier the behavior looks. Except with age, the stakes are much more costly and higher. Take your pick among pornography, affairs, anger, food, alcohol, overspending, or a host of other impulse control issues we can't seem to beat. An adult man should be able to say *no* to himself, but he doesn't have the power *in himself.* Silly.

In one corner of his life is the impulsive voice. You know him. Half the time you are already knee-deep into a behavior before you realize it's probably not the best thing to do. This voice is a driving force in our lives for a long time and knows us well. Want to know why? *He is you!* He's the "old man," the mole who works from inside the organization to sabotage your best intentions to defeat a behavior or habit that you know is not healthy for your relationship with the Holy Spirit or with the ones you love. He is a man of the moment, and once an idea to gratify him appears, stopping to pause, ask questions, or consider the consequences is not an option. The boy—another name for our old sin nature—doesn't like to think too hard about anything, especially if it fits into the category of self-gratification. He knows that the enemy of self-gratification is *to think ahead of time about an action.*

At that moment, when you may want to think about a decision, the boy turns on the big luminous high-definition billboard in your brain and flashes messages like these: "Hey, you deserve it!" "This is what men do!" "One more time for old time's sake!" "Why not?" "No one cares about it anyway!" "You can close the window if someone comes!" "God will forgive you!" "You negotiated a great deal!" "You need this!" And my personal favorite: "God wants you to be happy, right?"

I call this voice the Little Lawyer. He has airtight logic for every bad decision I make and is the inspiration for the mind games I play to rationalize doing or saying the wrong thing. The boy, the Little Lawyer, and the sin nature are one and the same, and they will never ask you to pause before deciding or tell you the facts about the bad decision

> *I call this voice the Little Lawyer. He has airtight logic for every bad decision.*

you are considering. These guys and Satan have been buddies since the Garden of Eden. (Again, see my book *Fight* for more on this axis of evil and how to conquer it.)

The bottom line: these embedded terrorists don't want you to become *a man.*

As a result, urges, impulses, and anxieties win the moment with qualities like inconsistency and questionable integrity. When faced with aggravation, pressure, isolation, or stress, the boy makes our number one temptation out to be our number one solution. Our ability to endure waiting or to delay self-gratification without becoming annoyed, mad, or upset is severely diminished. We get angry, guilty, and confrontational.

The main reason we devolve emotionally is because we get pimped like a common prostitute: we are promised that doing a particular thing will fulfill our need. So we bite down on this lie like a largemouth bass and offer our body as a slave to the behavior, attitude, or action. Then, after we take the bait and act out destructively, we are cast out to deal with the shame, dirtiness, or consequences of having to repair our relationships with God and people.

This practice of listening to the boy in me deepens my despair and self-loathing. How do I know? I've been pimped a few times in my day. Worst of all, the pimp is me!

Fighting against the pimp, of course, is the Holy Spirit. And when it comes to the issue of self-control, once again, the mission of the Spirit of Truth is to intervene, pull us aside, call us out, encourage us, and empower us to win the battle of self-rule.

The way the Holy Spirit gets this done initially is the same way I did it with Ryan, the same way any good dad grows a son: "But speaking the truth in love, we are to grow up in all *aspects* into Him who is the head, even Christ" (Ephesians 4:15, NASB). In other words, the Spirit says: "You know that behavior you have going on? Yes, the one that makes you look and feel small, immature, and out of control? The one you play all the mind tricks with yourself to justify? The one that conveniently makes you not deal with the man in the mirror? The one you reserve for your own private control away from My rule? Yeah, *that one!* Well, I want you to know, that's not what a man does, and it's time to grow up. You just have to decide that's what *you* want."

Every God's Man moving forward in Christ has had many ear-pulling conversations like this with the Holy Spirit. The Holy Spirit is after maturity in all aspects and in every area of our life. The apostle Paul, a great example of this ongoing work in a man's life, reflected on the process: "When I was a child, I *talked* *Think about it: the first thing a child lacks is self-control.*

like a child, I *thought* like a child, I *reasoned* like a child. *When I became a man, I put childish ways behind me*" (1 Corinthians 13:11). He was a boy once. His process of becoming a man involved a strong decision to move forward into maturity by thinking and acting differently. And now, as God's Man, he is starting that process over spiritually.

Think about it: the first thing a child lacks is self-control. Ever seen an arching-back temper tantrum? Ever seen your child have a meltdown in the grocery store line? Ever seen a brother punch his sister for taking his toy? Ever seen a child run away from his mom or dad and straight into a wall? You get the picture. No impulse control.

The champion of self-control in your life is the Holy Spirit, and when He has control of your mind, He causes you to be patient, to pause, and to consider the consequences of actions.

When a man is able to stop and say, "I don't have to have that, I don't have to do that, I don't have to say that, I don't have to think that, I don't have to eat that, I don't have to drink that, I don't have to click that, I don't have to see that, I don't have to touch that, I don't have to buy that, or I don't have to listen to that," he is growing up in all aspects in Christ through the power and process of the Holy Spirit in his life. What process, you ask? One that should be familiar to every God's Man.

> ## soar fact
> *When you are filled with, cooperating with, and taking in truth from the Holy Spirit, your ability to control your own behavior makes the turn toward manhood in dramatic ways.*

The Holy Spirit changes the way we make decisions by intervening in the exact spots that the pimp (the sinful nature) skips conveniently over when faced with a temptation. The pimp says, "Don't think about these things ahead of time and make a plan to avoid them." The Holy Spirit says, "Think about what you are going to do if confronted with that temptation again and make a plan." The pimp is the king of stimulus-response.

The Holy Spirit is the champion of the stimulus...pause...*new* response that honors God and shows love for people. His goal is to win you a pause so that you can consider the consequences or get out of there! The new insight and new truth the Holy Spirit gives you through the Word of God feeds a holy intuition, which strengthens your pause-ability and ability to be disciplined in the moment.

That is why fire stokers who dump more Bible into their relationship with the Holy Spirit build a wild fire of His influence and win more self-control. The pimp process leads to compulsive, impulsive, and out-of-control behaviors that dominate, enslave, and ruin, because it is based on saying yes to a lie. The Holy Spirit process, which produces a pause in between the stimulus and response, wins freedom through thoughtful consideration and a wise choice based on truth. "Me want" begins to lose out to "me gonna think this one through."

This battle to pause or not pause is the key to winning the battles you face over reactions and impulsive behaviors. Remember: pausing is synonymous with strength, or as Napoleon Bonaparte observed, "The strong man is the one who is able to intercept at will the communication between his senses and the mind."

Oui, monsieur. Napoleon couldn't have been more on the money. The only thing left is to stoke the fire of

> *"The strong man is the one who is able to intercept at will the communication between his senses and the mind."*

the Holy Spirit on this issue by getting some simple thoughts from Him that help us win the war for freedom from destructive choices through self-control.

His Will Is Your Power

A higher allegiance is synonymous with higher levels of discipline.

In the end, every man will discipline himself in the direction of his strongest hope. To get the girl, we discipline ourselves to buy flowers, write sappy cards, and concentrate on listening. Why? We hope to win her affections. To get the contracts for our business, we network, smile and dial, and follow up on leads. Why? We hope to get paid. To get that six-pack stomach (not me), we discipline ourselves to eat right and suffer a thirty-minute core workout at the gym. Why? We hope to look like the dude on the cover of *Men's Health*.

The Bible says that the secret to self-control and discipline is having a hope that transcends all other desires and temptations to give in or give up. We see this principle in Scripture as one God's Man teaching another how to stay disciplined in the faith:

> *Endure hardship* with us like a good soldier of Christ Jesus. No one serving as a *soldier* gets involved in civilian affairs—he *wants to please his commanding* officer. Similarly, if anyone competes as an *athlete,* he does not receive the *victor's crown* unless he competes according to the rules. The hardworking *farmer* should be the *first to receive a share* of the crops. *Reflect* on what I am saying, for *the Lord will give you insight* into all this. (2 Timothy 2:3–7)

The soldier, athlete, and farmer are each enticed to give in to a temptation. The soldier is tempted by civilian life. The athlete is tempted to cut corners (steroids). The farmer is tempted to sleep in. But each also has a strong hope waiting for him that is stronger than the temptation, which causes him to discipline himself and practice self-control. The soldier's hope is to win the approval of his commanding officer, so he concentrates on his military duty. The athlete's hope is a gold medal, so he follows the rules of competition. The farmer's hope is the upcoming harvest, so he wakes up early and

> *In the end, every man will discipline himself in the direction of his strongest hope.*

walks behind smelly oxen while plowing his field. When the stimulus of temptation comes to these three guys, their hope intervenes, and they say no to their temptation and yes to their hope.

Hope is power. And the Holy Spirit's mission in our life is to remind us of our strongest hope:

* The person of Jesus Christ
* The cross of Jesus Christ
* Eternity with Jesus Christ

What's more, Jesus Himself gave us His personal assurance that if we discipline ourselves and our choices for Him, He will give us the very thing, feeling, comfort, or object we gave up. Specifically, He said, "But *seek first* his kingdom and his righteousness, and *all these things will be given to you as well*" (Matthew 6:33). Jesus, through His indwelling presence in us through the Holy Spirit, continues daily to say "seek first his kingdom" to the man of God at the crossroads of temptation. The pimp says the opposite: "Seek self-gratification or else you are going to miss out on all these things. Hurry!" One is the strong hope of the person and promise of Jesus Christ. The second offers the promise of a broken relationship with the Holy Spirit and bondage.

Jesus says that God's will is your power. Self-control is synonymous with the strong hope of the kingdom of God and His will being done in and through you. Self-control is the difference between a willing spirit and a weak flesh, good intentions for God and consistent actions for God. The difference between impulse reactions and intu-

> *Hope is power. And the Holy Spirit's mission in our life is to remind us of our strongest hope.*

ition that pauses is simply this: Who is at the center of your hope? And who is making the promise? Jesus said, "For *whoever* does the *will* of my *Father* in heaven is my brother" (Matthew 12:50).

Armed with the strong hope of God's will in his mind, God's Man rises above all temptation. We speak our hope directly at the temptation, just as Jesus did, saying, "It is written…" during His temptation in the wilderness (read Luke 4). Satan and the pimp are defeated by the utterance of the will of God under the leadership of the Holy Spirit. The boy is no more, and a man rises to takes his place to stand guard in that domain of life forever:

- A man thinking about his purpose
- A man thinking humbly about his temptations and not borrowing trouble
- A man thinking ahead to remove pressures on himself
- A man who is ready to run when ambushed by opportunity
- A man who is suited up for his hour in history

Do this, knowing the time, that it is already the hour for you to awaken from sleep; for now salvation is nearer to us than when we believed. The night is

almost gone, and the day is near. Therefore let us lay aside the deeds of darkness
and put on the armor of light. Let us behave properly as in the day, not in
carousing and drunkenness, not in sexual promiscuity and sensuality, not in
strife and jealousy. But put on the Lord Jesus Christ, and make no provision for
the flesh in regard to its lusts. (Romans 13:11–14, NASB)

God's Men are donning armor, walking in the light, and suffocating the impulses
contrary to their hope in Christ. The Holy Spirit is making men out of boys for the
Lord Jesus in every age so that the will of God can go forward in every age. And just
as it would be ridiculous to see a grown man sucking his thumb in public, a slave to
a childish behavior, so the Enemy has made a mockery of God's Men by enslaving
them to the habits of boys. Together, with one firm voice, we must speak the words
of war to our ancient foe: "It ends here!"

*Holy Spirit, let the fight begin within me to grow up into all aspects of my faith. I
am done acting like a boy and accept Your call to self-control. Help me to respect
Your voice that is giving me chances to grow up and into the Christlikeness You have
waiting for me. I want to work with You. I want to be mature and complete. I
want to let go of childish ways of thinking and acting that say "boy" and not "man"
of God. I give You permission to confront me as a man. Please help me gain self-rule
over my behavior through Your control over my actions. I am done borrowing trouble.
It ends here and now.*

*Slow me down, Holy Spirit, long enough to win a pause and consider my
actions. Help me to reject all thoughts that justify impulse at the expense of my
faith. I am done being pimped by the sin nature within. I reject
his voice in the name of Jesus, and I accept Your voice as
the ruling one from this moment forward. Suffocate all
impulses that do not honor You. Help me turn up the
volume on Your will and voice by soaking my mind
in Your Word every day. Thank You for reminding
me of my future and my hope in Jesus, which is
stronger than any temptation. Keep me seeking that
first, moment to moment, today and every day. Amen.*

the rock vs. the hard place

To increase your effectiveness, make your emotions subordinate to
your commitments.

—Brian Koslow

It was one moment in time.

The classroom noise was reaching a fever pitch, and as the teacher, Kevin would have
to play bad cop again. His physical size and reputation made that task easier for him
and belied the good heart beneath his menacing exterior. Tribal tattoos on a high
school teacher? Yup.

Talk about working a tough room. A different mentality and stomach were needed
in this neck of the teaching world. This was a class for teenagers who already proved
that they didn't want anything to do with class.

"All right…all right…all right," Kevin bellowed as he stood to take command of
the misfits, as they were affectionately labeled in teachers' circles. As Kevin passed
through the aisles, dealing out the review sheet for Friday's history exam, he explained: "This test is half your grade, and if you want to pass this class, you need to
pay attention starting *now*." This shot across the bow was followed up by a head-
snapping comment about how not passing would mean summer school. Now everybody got quiet and began trying to listen.

Kevin noticed a couple of holdouts in the back texting on their cell phones, oblivious to him, the events around them, and the approaching hulk of a teacher. He interrupted their digital conversations by declaring, "I'll take those, please. Thank you very much." Then he seamlessly finished the thought he had begun expressing earlier: "And eighty percent of this test will be on the Civil War, so know the main battles, the players, and their importance to the causes of North and South. I am going to let you have the whole period to begin building answers for your review sheet. So take out your books and get to work. If you have any questions, come to my desk."

As he sat down, he inhaled deeply and exhaled gratefully for the breathing room afforded to him by having an in-class review day. The unrelenting challenges of his classroom, student issues, and pressures at home were sitting on his chest like an eight-hundred-pound gorilla. More important, he could feel himself slipping back into old habits and destructive ways of thinking because of the stress. It was little things. He was shorter and more defensive at home with his wife and daughter. His fuse was considerably shorter with the kids in the classroom, and he found himself quietly resenting their nonappreciation and lack of respect for teachers.

He was especially fond of the new cell phone and texting guidelines approved recently by the school board, which granted him complete authority to confiscate phones. Now *that* was fun. Something in him, something dark, liked to do this when the opportunity presented itself. He couldn't control a lot of things in his world, but at least, on this one point, he could pull the trigger and seize power in the situation.

His bad cop image was actually supported by the rules that served to blur the lines between a conscientious teacher and a control freak. What was not supported was taking this authority into his own hands and abusing it. What was not supported was violating his integrity for the sake of ego or for getting back at a student. What was not supported was compromising his ethics as a teacher and convictions as a Christian in the name of a joke.

A single moment in time changed all that and him forever.

Getting some empty space in his schedule for the day was a mixed blessing. He had a free hour, no papers to grade, and a classroom full of students working away on the review sheet (or doing their best doodling). He also had those two cell phones in front of him, one of which was now vibrating on his desk with a flashing and luminous screen that read "NEW MESSAGE" with a name underneath, revealing the identity of the person who was texting his student.

Instead of just tossing the phones in the top-right drawer as he usually did, Kevin left them on his desk and, in doing so, left himself open to a temptation: snooping into a student's private life. He looked at the screen again and thought about the wisdom of a teacher's reading a private text of a student. His thinking twisted like this: *In case anything happened, I could say that I was teaching the kid the importance of the message (which will be juvenile) versus the importance of studying to pass a test.* That sounded really good, and Kevin clicked the "Read" button on the phone.

Now he was through the door. There was no turning back.

What Kevin saw on the screen was a highly personal message from his student's love interest. While appalled at what he was doing, the voyeuristic opportunity to look into someone else's private life felt too good to miss. So Kevin kept reading, and with every word he felt dirty, stupid, and intrigued—all at once. The musings and passions of young love reminded him of happier times, free of the responsibilities of adult life. Now Kevin was clicking back through the messages in his student's in-box to get the scoop on today's text. The moment was turning deadlier by the second as the first transgression and emotional high of violating someone's privacy spawned an even creepier idea: respond to the message!

After all of one minute and forty seconds, a respected teacher without a blemish on his record was about to enter the world of a sixteen-year-old student and play a twisted prank on her and her boyfriend! Forget about the fact there would be only one person to blame for this joke. Forget about the ethics of it. Forget about whether or not God would approve. Forget about being God's Man.

Text away, Kevin!

A week later, after the student had filed a formal complaint and Kevin had been dismissed from his job, placed on unpaid administrative leave, and put under a formal investigation to determine if he would keep his teaching credentials, I ran into him. I had been following his journey as a man, husband, and father for three years, advising him to accept responsibility for his life, marriage, and family to do what *a man does*. His willingness to take responsibility and ownership, as well as to apply my counsel from Scripture, had been courageous and prompt. In Kevin I witnessed a solid transformation and the donation of countless hours to serve people less fortunate. He was right on track in so many ways.

Then, with Kevin at an emotional low, the Enemy came to test God's Man. Working with the compromiser (the sin nature), Satan made a hangman's noose (that innocent text message) look like a jump rope, and said, "It's easy. Come and play." Kevin let go of reason, violated his own identity, and was made unfaithful to deep convictions by the power *of a changing mood*.

It was a moment he'll never get back.

Testing Our Loyalty

Kevin morphed.

He went from God's Man who happens to teach to Teacher Man entitled to some "innocent" fun and payback. I call this "identity flipping." That's when, in a moment, we are persuaded to take off our identity in Christ in order to gratify the desires of our sinful nature, to gain acceptance by men, to meet a need outside the will of God, or to behave inconsistently with our faith. Some of us end up winning the moment while others do not.

God allows these moments to happen to test and develop us or expose and discipline us in our walk with Christ. Kevin was in good company. Think Job and Peter, Joseph and Daniel, David and the apostle Paul. This last duo actually have their personal thoughts about God's testing and development program recorded permanently in Scripture.

David said, "I know, my God, that you test the heart and are pleased with integrity" (1 Chronicles 29:17). He also recorded a prayer that recognized the tension of learning through testing and the need for power in the moment: "Teach me your way, O LORD, and I will walk in your truth; give me an undivided heart, that I may fear your name" (Psalm 86:11). David knew the difference in the moment between information ("teach me your way") and application ("and I will walk in your truth"). He also knew that faithfulness in the moment required supernatural help ("give me an undivided heart") and a heightened sense of accountability to his identity as God's Man ("that I may fear your name"). David wanted to be found faithful in his moments of testing.

Paul, too, was in touch with the spiritual reality that this life presents ongoing tests sponsored by God that "prove out" our faithfulness to Him. In fact, he used God's testing process to help reinforce his credibility with those he was seeking to influence for Christ. Only a severely tested man could be this bold:

> We had previously *suffered* and been insulted in Philippi, *as you know,* but *with the help of our God we dared to tell you* his gospel in spite of *strong opposition.* For the appeal we make does not spring from error or *impure motives,* nor are we trying to trick you. On the contrary, we speak as men *approved by God* to be *entrusted* with the gospel. We are not trying to please men but *God, who tests our hearts.* (1 Thessalonians 2:2–4)

Paul's overriding point? We had some moments of severe testing and passed, baby! So when you look at and listen to us, remember that we are not in this thing to make an impression or take advantage of anybody. To make sure of that, God put us in the fire to test our commitment and motives, to see if we would live for an audience of one. God is on us every step of the way, testing our faithfulness.

> *A man must be proven by being put into situations that call for courage.*

Paul knew that men respect other men who are willing to be tested, are tested, and come through it without compromising or selling out to circumstances, various pressures, or their feelings. A man must be proven by being put into situations that call for courage, or in Paul's case, faithfulness to Christ under pressure.

We also call them rites of passage. God does not advance or promote leaders without this type of analysis, testing, and assessment of how we handle ourselves in private, away from the spotlight, in the recesses of our heart. God's examinations of His men are intentionally rigorous and specific to the man, but at the same time, all tests are intended to eliminate impurity of commitment, expose the substance of faith, and develop a stronger hope and witness.

The Holy Spirit is in you to help you pass these tests. His goal? Life-specific faithfulness in you and through you as you seek to live out the life God has called you to live moment by moment. Versus what? Versus the life you think you are entitled to live, in the moment, based on changes of circumstance, mood, or fortunes. The Holy Spirit knows how tempting and easy it is for men to compartmentalize behavior in a moment based on a prevailing frame of mind, vibe, atmosphere, or need in our life. That's why the Holy Spirit's most important mission is to develop your strong *identity* as God's Man, increase your *responsibility* to God's will, and grow your *ability* to live God's way under pressure.

This is called faithfulness, and it is the most appreciated, celebrated, and contested fruit of the Spirit in the basket. Why is that? The opposite of faithfulness is unfaithfulness, better known to God as idolatry.

Feelings for Faith

Identity is to faithfulness what feelings are to idolatry. Let me explain. Faithfulness is the only character quality strong enough to defeat our moods or feelings in our moments of crisis and testing. It is the one thing required when we meet a command or priority of God and *don't want to do it*. Yes, you read that right. God's best men sometimes find themselves not *wanting* to do God's will but still transcend their feelings and pressures through faithfulness. In the end, you see their identity in God pushing them past their feelings and toward faithfulness.

Think of Jesus in the Garden of Gethsemane, the prospect of the cross before Him, and the emotional turmoil He found Himself in. He didn't *want* to do it, but He was faithful.

Think of Moses being called to have it out with Pharaoh. He definitely didn't *want* to do it, but he was faithful.

Think of Hosea getting told by God to reconcile with his adulteress wife and to "love her as the LORD loves the

> *Identity is to faithfulness what feelings are to idolatry.*

Israelites, though they turn to other gods" (Hosea 3:1). Every fiber of his being didn't *want* to do that (especially in that culture), but he was faithful to God by ransoming Gomer back and loving her as God commanded.

Eleven of the twelve disciples were called by God to meet death by martyrdom. Same for the apostle Paul and many of the church's first converts. Wanted to? Not a chance. Faithful? Of course. That's why we name our kids Matthew, Mark, Luke, John, Peter, James, Stephen, Paul, Andrew, Timothy, Philip, and Thomas. To the very end, by the power of the Holy Spirit, not one of them violated their identity as God's Man through compromise.

The same Holy Spirit lives in you and wants to build the same story of faithfulness for your testimony before God and man. *All* God's Men are tested for faithfulness.

It is called a healthy sense of duty to your identity.

This means He will have you consider two things in every moment of testing you will ever face. First, He will move you to remember your identity as a son of God and insist on faithfulness to your sonship. The Holy Spirit will say emphatically, "You are a Christian! You are a follower of Jesus. You are a child of the living God."

Second, He will ask you to sacrifice something you want in that moment for something of greater value connected to your faith—an action that requires faith! Most of the time, this involves sacrificing your claim to some feeling that would be produced for you through unfaithfulness to God. Take your pick from one of these favorite feelings:

- Acceptance by others
- Physical gratification
- Revenge
- Being in charge
- Being right
- Deserving more
- Being independent from restraints
- Power over others
- Wanting justice

Saying no to these feelings is the stuff of a true Holy Spirit warrior. In every instance, the choice to sacrifice is a risk, with the Holy Spirit offering a later return on the investment of your faithful obedience to God's command. That's why God promises such outrageous rewards in heaven for those who are faithful to obey Him on earth. It costs us a lot.

Here are what some faithful guys do:

- Larry sacrifices competition for power in his relationship with his wife for connection and union.
- Bill sacrifices relaxing Thursday nights in front of the television so he can lead as his son's junior high Bible study.
- Tim sacrifices a tingle below his belt in front of the computer in order to love God with his mind and love his future wife.
- Doug sacrifices a new high-tech plasma television for the house in order to financially support a ministry to orphans in his community.
- Pete sacrifices enjoying a beer with the guys for the protection and encouragement of Ted, who is five days sober and still vulnerable.
- Jeff sacrifices his weekend off for a ministry to the homeless.
- Gary sacrifices his comfort zone and risks inviting a neighbor to church.

- My pastor sacrifices financially and materially to create more credibility and integrity in his ministry locally.

All of these are real men making real choices that say to God, "I will relate to You in the midst of my life on *Your terms* in spite of how I feel in the moment or in the moments of weakness."

The Holy Spirit is moving every God's Man to affirm his faith at the expense of his feelings by risking in God's direction on an increasing and more aggressive basis. Wherever you are, in whatever context, whoever you are with, and however it needs to get done, if you *perceive or know* something to be God's will in that situation, then sacrifice for it as the Holy Spirit leads. Practically, this means learning to develop a discipline of trusting the friendly voice of the Holy Spirit who calls you to faithfulness numerous times each day in your public and private domains.

> **soar fact**
> *Faithfulness is synonymous with sacrifice. When God's Man finds himself in the moment, sacrificing himself, his feelings, or his agenda, the Holy Spirit is strongly at work.*

Trusting the Holy Spirit's voice is synonymous with

- trusting the example of Jesus Himself.
- trusting the commands of God implicitly.
- trusting your conscience.
- trusting your intuition and experience as God's Man.
- trusting your biblical insight.
- trusting the conservative approach to situations or decision making that preserves your integrity with God and people.
- trusting the warnings connected to the consequences of disobedience to God in your life.
- trusting the counsel of a spiritual accountability partner.
- trusting the promises of God.
- trusting all directions that lead to more freedom and healing in your life.

Conversely, the Holy Spirit says to *never* trust a spiritually compromising thought *sponsored by a feeling*. Even when that feeling comes up with all sorts of goofy, self-serving logic, don't compromise your faith to gain a short-lived feeling.

The mission of the Holy Spirit in your life is to cause spontaneous or continuous spiritual fervor over things that matter to God. All of the following are signs the Holy Spirit is working in your life on a specific matter:

- You have conflicts internally.
- You are thinking twice about decisions.
- You are remembering the consequences of similar actions in the past.
- You are having cautionary dreams or consistent streams of thoughts that warn you of certain actions.
- Your internal radar is flashing red about certain people or situations.
- You are feeling unusually conflicted in certain environments.
- You are getting unsolicited but personally targeted advice direct from various sources (for example, a sermon this past weekend, a friend says the same thing, and then your Scripture reading for the day puts the nail in the coffin).

These are all called promptings. It is the equivalent of a loyal friend going, *"Psssssst,"* getting your attention, and motioning a certain direction, and then you listening without having to understand all the whys and whats of what is going on. All you know is that someone you trust is doing the asking, you are changing your course or line of thinking on the fly, and you are content to get the explanation or reasons for the concern later.

The Holy Spirit is in you to deliver *a faithful man to God*.

Now and Later

Faithfulness *now* is the Holy Spirit's guarantee of *later*. Listen closely to the "now and later" ministry of the Holy Spirit in your life:

Now it is God *who makes both us and you stand firm in Christ.* He anointed us, set his seal of ownership on us, and *put his Spirit in our hearts* as a deposit, guaranteeing what is to come. (2 Corinthians 1:21–22)

The Holy Spirit says to every believer: *I am in you to ensure the faithfulness and integrity of your conduct on earth by helping you to win moments, stand firm, and be faithful. I am also confirming your calling by commissioning and anointing you to defeat the sin and evil around you. And I am branding your soul with the burning-hot orange-and-red insignia of God* now *so there will be no dispute as to who you belong to* later on *before God.*

Here's the picture: standing firm now through the power of the Holy Spirit, empowered now to win faithfulness in the power of the Holy Spirit, scheduled for secure arrival later in heaven, marked and sealed by the Holy Spirit. All the bases are covered.

When I am placed between the rock of my commitment to Christ and a hard place of testing, one of two things will happen: I will be faithful or I will compromise. Those are the only two results. Either my emotions will be subordinate to my commitment to God or my commitment to God will be subordinate to my emotions. I will choose self-sacrifice or I will choose self-preservation. I will be God's Man or I will be my own man. Either I will be more assured and confident of my salvation to come or I will, through my compromising, be less assured and prone to fear.

> *Either my emotions will be subordinate to my commitment to God or my commitment to God will be subordinate to my emotions.*

Faithfulness will produce increasing measures of satisfaction, contentment, and peace in my life. Compromise will produce more regret, discontentment, and anxiety. Which behavior and consequences do you want right now? Exactly! That is why faithful, consistent, yielded, and immediate cooperation with the Holy Spirit sends a message to God that says: *I will live on Your terms.* Unfaithful resistance to the Holy Spirit sends a message to God that says: *You need to relate to me on my terms.*

Both now and later are the domain of the Holy Spirit in a man's life. He cannot keep the faith apart from the work of the Holy Spirit. Faithfulness comes from strong bonds, strong communication, and strong sensitivity to Holy Spirit leadership as God's Man fights the good fight now in anticipation of rewards later. He wants you to take the crown!

I have fought the good fight, I have finished the race, *I have kept the faith.* Now there is in store for me the crown of righteousness, which the Lord, the righteous Judge, will award to me on that day—and not only to me, but also to all who have longed for his appearing. (2 Timothy 4:7–8)

Smashing compromise is the desire of the Holy Spirit for all of His fighting men. As we have been learning, He is deeply engaged and active in the struggle against the compromiser within, winning more faithfulness for believers with each passing day. He's telling you to stand more boldly. He's moving in you to act more loyally. He's driving you to live more conscientiously as God's Man. He's helping you to see in yourself the difference between being interested in God versus being faithful to God. He is showing you that the self-interested man does things only when the right circumstances or feelings permit him. That's called being a boy.

At the same time, the Holy Spirit is also calling you to a higher version of yourself that rises above circumstances and feelings to be faithful to God *in the midst of pressure.* That's called being a man.

Shifts of fortune cannot change the commitment of the Spirit-filled man, and suffering is considered the fruit of our higher allegiance. Again, a man and a warrior think and act this way. Small acts of faithfulness add up, and it is in the little things that our fight begins. For it is in the small acts of obedience where true spiritual strength lies and the greatest preparation is made for the larger fights to come.

The Holy Spirit's mind on your faithfulness in the moments of testing is crystal clear: remember who you are!

> So do not throw away your confidence; it will be richly rewarded. You need to persevere so that *when you have done the will of God,* you will receive what he has promised. For in just a very little while, "He who is coming will come and will not delay. *But my righteous one will live by faith.* And if he shrinks back, I will not be pleased with him." But *we are not of those who shrink back* and are destroyed, but of those who believe and are saved. (Hebrews 10:35–39)

Our greatest source of spiritual confidence is remembering our identity as a son of God. When a Father says, "This is my Son, whom I love; with him I am well pleased" (Matthew 3:17), the fight for faithfulness is won. Sonship wins spiritual championships in the lives of God's Men. Throw that identity away, and your confidence in the moment goes with it.

You, as your own man, are simply not strong enough to resist powerful feelings that lead to compromising your faith.

That is why the mission of the Holy Spirit in your life is to pound that identity deep into your spirit:

> *The Holy Spirit is also calling you to a higher version of yourself that rises above circumstances and feelings to be faithful to God in the midst of pressure. That's called being a man.*

> Therefore, brothers, *we have an obligation*—but it is not to the sinful nature, to live according to it. For if you live according to the sinful nature, you will die; but if *by the Spirit you put to death the misdeeds of the body,* you will live, because *those who are led by the Spirit of God are sons of God.* For you did not receive a spirit that makes you a slave again to fear, but *you received the Spirit of sonship.* And by him we cry, "Abba, Father." The *Spirit himself testifies with our spirit that we are God's children.* Now if we are children, then we are heirs—heirs of God and co-heirs with Christ, *if indeed we share in his sufferings* in order that we may also share in his glory. (Romans 8:12–17)

Sonship is our brotherhood sponsored by the Holy Spirit. This is what sonship involves:

- A duty to represent the Father
- A higher allegiance in moments of testing
- A deadly mission against sin
- A willingness to be led by the Spirit of God
- A confidence in and closeness with the Father
- A continuous inner witness by the Holy Spirit as to our identity
- A commitment to sacrifice or suffer loss in order to remain faithful now with the hope for later glory as a son

Now and later we will be sons.

Holy Spirit, thank You for Your mission of sonship in my life. Keep witnessing that identity to me, that I am a son of God called to faithfulness. I want to win every encounter with the compromiser within, and I cannot do that without Your strong presence in me. Help me to focus on faithfulness in the little battles I face today, and help me to remember that this is where true spiritual strength is developed. Prepare me for my tests of faithfulness. I welcome them because I want to grow up and into Christlikeness. I want to pass more tests for Your glory. Use the tests I am experiencing today to eliminate the boy, along with any impurity of commitment, and to develop a stronger witness for God.

Holy Spirit, help me to push past feelings and into commitment on a consistent basis. Thank You that I am not expected to like the hard choices to be faithful now, but I also am looking forward to Your rewarding those same choices later. Thank You for Your strong promise that helps me to respond to Your promptings in my life. Continue to get my attention. My ears are open to Your voice and witness today in me.

I am a son and I love You. Amen.

Part 3

transactions

peculiar power

The world has yet to see what God can do with and for and through
and in and by the man who is fully and wholly consecrated to Him.
I will try my utmost to be that man.

—D. L. Moody

A stunning release of power.

The sound of the explosion was heard up to three thousand miles away. That is
on-the-ground intel after the 1883 Krakatoa volcano eruption in Indonesia. More
scientifically, the Volcanic Explosivity Index (VEI) was a six, which rates the explosion as "colossal" or unusually and impressively large.

In terms of raw power, this baby was as imposing as it was inspiring. The scale of
impact, the range of impact, and the degree to which this volcano affected the globe
has never been matched in modern times.

Here are a few mind-blowing facts surrounding this explosion of power:

- Volcanic ash from the explosion fell on the decks of ships sixteen hundred
  miles away.
- The explosion itself was heard over one-third of the earth's surface, beginning in Indonesia and echoing across the planet's surface as far as Australia

and to Rodriques Island, which is one thousand miles east of Madagascar.
A "distant roar of cannons" was how people described the sound.

- The atmospheric shock waves (recorded by barographs worldwide) circled
the earth seven times over the next five days.

- Ash rose over fifty miles into the atmosphere.

- Spectacular red-sky sunsets were reported in the United States and Europe
for the next three years, due to sunlight reflecting off the ash particles.

- A volcanic dust veil acted as a solar-radiation filter that caused dropping
global temperatures and changed worldwide climatology for the next five
years.

- The explosive energy of the Krakatoa event was the equivalent of 150 mega-
tons of TNT (150 million tons).[4]

My mom had a term for this kind of thing: *Ay caramba!*

The world had to deal with the repercussions of an event 150 times more powerful
than the atom bomb dropped on Hiroshima in 1945! The scientific reality behind all
the effects of the volcano is connected to the displacement volume of an explosive
event. In everyday terms, we refer to this as a blast zone. Krakatoa's blast zone was so
unusually large because of a unique event within the volcano that occurred during
the "normal" explosion.

In essence, *something got inside it.*

As the volcano's walls began to rupture after the first two explosions, ocean water
entered the magmatic chambers creating the conditions for a phreatomagmatic event
(a volcanic eruption caused by contact between magma and ground water in which
the water, gases, and steam combine to create an explosion). This was the secret
power behind Krakatoa's unusual force and displacement power. The mother of all
pressure cookers was created, contained, and then carried outward at the moment
when *the power inside overcame the pressure outside.*

The result was a superexplosion that literally rocked the world.

What Has Gotten into You?

What do phreatomagmatic volcanic events, Krakatoa, the Holy Spirit, and rocking the world have to do with God's Men today?

Everything.

I touched on it earlier, but let's review. As we make *transitions* in our thinking about the Holy Spirit from the ethereal and impersonal to the personal and practical (part 1), as we cooperate with Him in the specific transformations He desires to achieve in us by subduing the sinful nature (the boy) and creating a man having the character of Christ (part 2), and as we now focus on the powerful works the Holy Spirit seeks to accomplish through us, we must reflect seriously on the nature and power of the explosive transactions that come from the synergy of His power and our faith.

What we see biblically is that, properly embraced, the work of the Holy Spirit is no ordinary explosion of God's power. Look again at how Jesus Himself predicted the displacement factor of men under the influence of the Holy Spirit as told in the book of Acts:

> "What you'll get is the Holy Spirit. And *when the Holy Spirit comes on you, you will be able to be my witnesses* in Jerusalem, all over Judea and Samaria, even to *the ends of the world.*"
>
> These were his last words. As they watched, he was taken up and disappeared in a cloud. They stood there, staring into the empty sky. Suddenly two men appeared—in white robes! They said, "You Galileans!—*why do you just stand here looking up at an empty sky*? This very Jesus who was taken up from among you to heaven will come as certainly—and mysteriously—as he left."
> (Acts 1:8–11, MSG)

A turning point in world history loomed. Something was about to happen that would reverberate out of Jerusalem and be felt worldwide. Jesus's leaving was a first and necessary explosion the disciples *had to feel.* The walls of their personal expectations (that Jesus would build a physical kingdom on earth) would finally collapse by His ascension, making way for a flooding entry of the Holy Spirit. In other words, an emotional low in the disciples and a power from on high were about to coalesce, establishing the perfect conditions for a Spirit-induced explosion of power that would send shock waves over the entire planet for centuries to come.

> *Something was about to happen that would reverberate out of Jerusalem and be felt worldwide.*

The boiling hopes, the magmatic expectations, and the powerful attachments of the disciples over the last three years were ruptured *intentionally* by God, leaving a gaping hole of opportunity *in them.* Soon the floodgates opened, and the Holy Spirit entered and flooded every cavity of their soul with His assurance and anointing for ministry. As they waited in that upper room in Jerusalem, living water suddenly inundated their souls, rapidly mixing with and making perfect sense of all their anticipations, prospects, and probabilities connected to their relationship with Jesus. All the dots were connected, and the lid of their willingness to be used for God's purpose was blown off. So powerful was the initial explosion of spiritual energy created by the Holy Spirit that those who witnessed it were at a complete loss. Something had clearly entered, possessed, and fully taken over the bodies and minds of these men. But what? Someone had to explain this spectacle of exploding men.

That's when Peter stood up and, backed by the other eleven, spoke out with bold urgency: "Fellow Jews, all of you who are visiting Jerusalem, listen carefully and get this story straight. These people aren't drunk as some of you suspect. They haven't had time to get drunk—it's only nine o'clock in the morning. This is what the prophet Joel announced would happen:

"In the Last Days," God says,
"I will pour out my Spirit
    on every kind of people:
Your sons will prophesy,
    also your daughters;
Your young men will see visions,
    your old men dream dreams.

When the time comes,
    I'll pour out my Spirit
On those who serve me, men and women both,
    and they'll prophesy.
I'll set wonders in the sky above
    and signs on the earth below,
Blood and fire and billowing smoke,
    the sun turning black and the moon blood-red,
Before the Day of the Lord arrives,
    the Day tremendous and marvelous;
And whoever calls out for help
    to me, God, will be saved." (Acts 2:14–21, MSG)

Peter described a spiritual movement caused by the explosive, visible, and world-altering power of the Holy Spirit invading the souls of 120 men to advance the kingdom of God.

This is the end game of the Holy Spirit and the moment we have been building to in our journey together in *Soar.* The message from Peter then and from me now is that the Holy Spirit has designs on your moment in time, in your personal context, for your blast zones of influence, and He wants to work through you in *culturally powerful ways* to make a difference.

At Pentecost the most meaningful thing that could happen in *that context* was for men to speak in discernible languages, praising God in ways that stunned people who were visiting from all over the world. Watch the film:

> Now there were staying in Jerusalem God-fearing Jews from every nation under heaven. When they *heard this sound,* a crowd came together in bewilderment, because each one heard them speaking in his own language. Utterly amazed, they asked: "Are not all these men who are speaking Galileans? Then how is it that each of us hears them in his own native language?" (Acts 2:5–8)

Utter amazement.

Now my question for you and me is, What work of the Holy Spirit in me, and in the group of men I am in community with, would absolutely shock the people of my culture, help others to see God, and foster a sense of wonder over the power responsible for this?

Our times are unprecedented in human history. Much like our brother disciples of the first century, the global community of God's Men worldwide is being turned upside down by events out of our control. Through technology, the world is sitting on our porch. The earth below the world's feet is shaking as economies collapse and entire countries implode. Personal dreams are being ruptured. Expectations of the future are being altered. Reality is biting. And because of technology, everybody's backyard is a cell phone screen away, and *we can watch what is happening to everyone else!*

Think about the 2009 elections in Iran. Even in a closed country like Iran, what was once an invisible movement to the rest of the world was seen and experienced all over the world in real time. The benefit of Pentecost was the ability by a visiting world to see a movement in real time. The venue today is not a gathering of thousands in one city but of billions of technology users who can see and hear exactly what is happening on any day in any part of the planet. The situational dynamics of that first Pentecost and initial blast zone of the kingdom are now ours in these last days. But will the sleeping giant—God's Men—rise up, wait upon the Holy Spirit, get filled, and explode into their world?

Like the disciples, many of God's Men are disillusioned, staring at the sky, waiting for the life they want to appear. And while I am no angel dressed in white, I am your brother, and I am here to say to all men who name His name worldwide:

> *God's Men! Why are you standing there looking into the sky? Leave yesterday behind.*
> *Jesus is coming back! It is not a time for standing still. It is a time to go into prayer*
> *with your brothers, to wait eagerly and expectantly, to get soaked in the Holy Spirit,*
> *and to release the power in you to your waiting and watching world!*

Just as the world was ripe in the first century for an explosion of power through God-filled men, enabled and equipped by the Holy Spirit, the global dynamics of change and challenge are percolating an all-inclusive, culturally transcendent harvest of the Spirit not seen since the days of Pentecost. Something happened in that upper room that changed the landscape of the spiritual world forever, motivating men to do things never before seen. Spirit-filled male culture led the way, spawning cross-cultural movements of evangelism, church growth, local ministry, and missions that span the world. The Spirit's mission was arranged *by God* and *for God* for that hour, just as Jesus predicted.

What was that mission? To rock their world.

Rock Your World

The image was of water—a familiar one. To a first-century Jewish believer, baptism meant the same thing it does today: getting soaked. A complete and total covering of water physically represented a spiritual oneness with whatever message called for the baptism. John's message was repentance. So getting baptized by John meant you intended to change your ways.

When Jesus said that John the Baptist's *outer* baptism would be matched by an *inner* baptism by the Holy Spirit, the men of Galilee knew a couple things: *no part of their life would be spared, and a fundamental change of their nature would occur as a result.* A fuller and deeper identification with His person and message was on the horizon. A powerful inner

> Get this: somebody's waiting on your personal outbursts of the Holy Spirit.

work was coming, to be followed by an equally powerful outburst of the Holy Spirit through them to be publicly witnessed and experienced by a waiting world.

As we learned in part 2 of this book, the same thing is happening to us right now through the transforming work of the Holy Spirit growing us up into all aspects of Him. That's the powerful inner work but not the end game of that transformation. The Holy Spirit has an audience waiting for our eruption right now.

Get this: somebody's waiting on your personal outbursts of the Holy Spirit.

The baptism and fullness of the Spirit *in your life* is intended to produce a witness in *your world.* We are going to dive into the practical expressions of what that means in these final chapters. But for now, we must simply see and accept the responsibility of being used by the Holy Spirit to create a blast zone of impact in the Jerusalems, Judeas, Samarias, and far-out places of His choosing. The book of Acts is still being written, *and you're part of it,* because the Holy Spirit has not changed His ways. All the gifts of the Holy Spirit are still available to Him to allocate to whomever, whenever, and wherever on the planet that He desires, just as He did with the first disciples.

Without entering into a big discussion, we can all agree on one thing: He decides who gets what gifts for His purposes. And we also know that to ensure our unity, no man receives *all the gifts* from this baptism of Spirit. We are allotted *some* of the gifts of the Spirit in order to make us reliant on the body of Christ, interdependent, and needing each other to experience the fullness of God. *This diversity of gifting is a good thing and keeps us connected.*

For now, the reminder is sufficient: *you have been given gifts from the Holy Spirit that others do not have,* which makes you very important, my brotha! You have been shaped uniquely for a specific impact today, and it is your responsibility to discern and determine what spiritual gifts the Holy Spirit has deposited in you and put them to work now in your world:

> There are different kinds of gifts, but the same Spirit. There are different kinds of service, but the same Lord. There are different kinds of working, but the same God works all of them in all men.
> Now to each one the manifestation of the Spirit is given for the common good. (1 Corinthians 12:4–7)

The book of Acts catalogs the moments of ignition when men became dangerously effective agents of the Holy Sprit's power by using the gifts He had given them. Shoulder to shoulder, before the same thousands of people they'd hidden from only weeks earlier, these guys went public for Jesus multiple times. Through the power of the Holy Spirit, they

- touched the untouchable and healed many.
- pressed the fight and accepted the cost of being messengers of the good news.
- stayed faithful in spite of heavy opposition from men in their culture wanting to stop the cause of Christ.
- led thousands of people in church.

> ### soar fact
> *The Holy Spirit is never deposited inside of a man for the sole purpose of remaining there. His mission is to engage the world through yielded and gifted men ready to sacrifice their personal dream for God's revealed will.*

- taught, organized, served, encouraged, and equipped Christians.
- identified needs and assigned other men to care for the needs of widows and orphans.
- raised up men "known to be full of the Spirit and wisdom" (Acts 6:3) and turned over new ministries to these men.
- died for the cause of the gospel.
- planted churches all over their world.
- were God's Men wherever, however, and under whatever circumstances to their last breath.

All of these exploits came after a season of disillusionment, discouragement, and defeat. Then the Holy Spirit came, baptized and filled them, and beautifully unleashed them on the waiting world.

It was the sound heard round the spiritual world.

Blast Zones

One transformed man transforms many things:

For if, by the trespass of the one man, death reigned through that one man, how much more will those who receive God's abundant provision of grace

and of the gift of righteousness reign in life through the one man, Jesus
Christ.

Consequently, just as the result of one trespass was condemnation for all
men, so also the result of one act of righteousness was justification that brings
life for all men. For just as through the disobedience of the one man the many
were made sinners, so also through the obedience of the one man the many
will be made righteous. (Romans 5:17–19)

The story of human history emanates directly out of the character and conduct of
two men: Adam and Jesus Christ. Their story is our story, and it is still being played
out today. Either men around the world are in Adam or men are in Jesus Christ.
Consequently, men are being either disobedient or obedient to God. Men are either
producing suffering or producing life for others. Either death is reigning or life and
health are being created.

Pick up a newspaper and track the suffering you see worldwide. It's a leadership
issue: the character of Adam or the character of Christ is prevailing in cultures
around the globe, producing conduct and choices that touch people in the blast
zones of their leadership.

A quick study of the headlines tells a tragic story of broken male leadership and
impact. Fatherlessness, domestic violence, rape, divorce, political corruption, sex traf-
ficking, prostitution, exploitation of the vulnerable, tribalism, greed, materialism, and
a plethora of power trips are just a few of the issues that stem from ungodly male
character gone wrong. Male culture and leadership styles influence every social, political, domestic, economic, and religious infrastructure worldwide. Sadly, millions of
God's Men *contribute* to the waves of suffering versus serving to *alleviate* the suffering
in their blast zones of influence. They are blending with their culture. The boy is
winning, and the voice of the Holy Spirit is muted in their lives.

The Holy Spirit is grieved as Christ's followers lose critical battles and injustice flows
unmitigated over millions around the world. People are suffering, and God is watching His boys do the damage: "The vineyard of the LORD Almighty is the house of

Israel, and the men of Judah are the garden of his delight. And he looked for justice, but saw bloodshed; for righteousness, but heard cries of distress" (Isaiah 5:7).

Then and now

- God is tracking the character and conduct of His men.
- God is looking to see His character (justice, compassion, and righteousness) reproduced in His men.
- God knows that character is expressed in conduct that will bring either health or harm to those connected to His men.
- God is tracking the influence of men for the sake of His name and for the sake of those hurt by their character and conduct.
- God will judge His sons severely for how they treat people (see Isaiah 5:8–30).
- God is a disappointed Father who does not wish to but must now chastise and discipline His own sons.

You and I have been given, for better or for worse, the ability to produce life and death through our character and conduct. The Holy Spirit took a group of men at Pentecost, saved

soar fact
Every man ever created has a blast zone of influence.

them, filled them, changed them inside, and turned them loose to bring His health and life to a waiting world. It was a movement in time through yielded men. It was a fresh movement, not of the letter or of stale religion, but of the Spirit who refreshed those who entered the blast zone and ignited life, God's Men knew this movement came from the inside out: "He has made us competent as ministers of a new covenant—not of the letter but of the Spirit; for the letter kills, but the Spirit gives life" (2 Corinthians 3:6).

Like the men who were a part of the first massive explosion of the Spirit in the book of Acts, you are not asked to do in your world what the Holy Spirit has not given you the character and power to accomplish. The Spirit wants your world rocked, and He is going to gift you with the power and show you exactly how to use it.

Something has gotten inside you. It's building in you. And it's just a matter of time before the eruption occurs. You have been dormant, but the transition to active has begun. The world is waiting.

Are you ready to accept and unleash the power?

> *Holy Spirit, thank You for coming to me through Christ, dwelling in me, and filling up my life with new gifts and a new purpose to replace old ways and old habits that didn't glorify God.*
>
> *I want You to baptize my hopes and dreams afresh with Your power. I want to ignite life and health in the world around me in the character of Christ. I want a blast zone of impact that causes others to wonder why a guy like me is doing the things I want to do for You. I want to be Your witness in my Jerusalem, Judea, Samaria, and wherever You choose to take me.*
>
> *Give me Your eyes so I can see all the opportunities before me on a moment-by-moment basis: big and small. This prayer is my flashpoint, my yielding to Your work in and, more important, through me now. Pour out Your Spirit upon me, in me, and through me. Holy Spirit, You have my permission and cooperation to create a spectacle through me for the global glory of God. I am Your servant. I ask this in the name of my Savior, Jesus. Amen.*

releasing captives

If your Gospel isn't touching others, it hasn't touched you!

—CURRY R. BLAKE

Every man has his "Egypts."

I call them Egypts now, but before I was a believer, they were simply circumstances, relationships, feelings, actions, and ways of seeing myself and others that made up my life without God. As a young man I felt like an accident.

My dad was depressed, distant, and very addicted. Mom was struggling to deal with an alcoholic husband and seven kids.

I was in the custody of school and friends.

I had no authority or accountability.

I was in a desperate search for an identity and connection.

I found other lost boys, and we banded together in Egypt.

Our Egyptian culture was one of parties, drinking, and escapades of vandalism in the name of fun.

God became a buzz kill you couldn't take seriously.

Sin was my greatest source of identity, relationship, comfort, and pleasure, so I chased it aggressively in all its pleasurable forms.

I called that "having a good time."

But in the quiet, usually when I lay down to go to sleep, there was that nagging sense, a faint whisper, that this was not who I really was, not what I really wanted to be doing, and not how I really wanted to live. The guilt, shame, pain, addiction, lies, headaches, bruises, black eyes, fears, and harm that I caused the people connected to my life in Egypt made me question my course—but usually not for long. To even think about another life would mean to give up a hard-won identity and the acceptance from others that I craved, as well as rejecting a lifestyle that possessed all of my most important relationships. Besides, no one ever explained to me why I felt this battle inside, told me what it involved, or showed me a way out. How does a man save himself from the only life he knows?

He doesn't.

But on a fateful summer night in July 1982, on the heels of some hard partying with friends, I decided to give that small voice inside some liberty and let it explore with me the possibility of life outside of Egypt. I decided to see if there was another identity for me, another way to be, another world with other connections to God and people out there. But where should I go with my questions? Who could give me the answers? Who had the knowledge?

Amazingly, without much reflection and a naive boldness, I started banging on Jesus's door and asking for a personal audience. No answer. So I banged on the door again, saying, "I want to see You." No answer. Undeterred, I kept saying this until a very warm and unusual presence blanketed my body and permeated my room. Imagine the sensation of warm water flooding over your head, neck, and shoulders after being in a cold pool. This felt amazing, so much so that I found myself weeping uncontrollably. It was the feeling of freedom.

Jesus answered the door, but in hindsight, the truth was that He was the one who had been knocking on mine! It just took me a long time to open it. In one shot, I cried out to Jesus in my room, welcomed His presence into my life, and was baptized in the Holy Spirit. It wasn't the upper room of the disciples; it was the back room of my parents' place. What happened exactly? Jesus Christ stamped my passport, signaling a border crossing into a new country. Good-bye Egypt. Welcome to the kingdom of God.

That night was my burning bush, my personal Exodus, and my Pentecost.

The next day I was glowing from the inside out, and people did not know what to make of me, especially my close friends. Harder for them to swallow was the fact that my desire for drugs, partying, and things related had been incinerated without logical explanation.

I didn't go to a church service, revival meeting, or Billy Graham crusade. I simply came out of the back room a

> *That night was my burning bush, my personal Exodus, and my Pentecost.*

different man, telling a simple story similar to the blind man who said candidly to those who asked: "One thing I do know. I was blind but now I see" (John 9:25).

I have told thousands the same story I just relayed to you above with few, if any, changes. The Holy Spirit floodgate had been opened, and living water was running through my mind and life at five million cubic feet of holy water per second. This was a Class 5 spiritual rapid and it was all I could do to hang on to so much purpose, wisdom, security, identity, family, vision, forgiveness, acceptance, love, affirmation, and newfound freedom without weeping or witnessing or both.

The details of your story of deliverance may differ, but all followers of Jesus share a common story of deliverance from spiritual darkness and sin into the light of Christ, the kingdom of God, and life in the Spirit. Whatever our spiritual tapestry, this is the silver thread that connects all of us to the black backdrop of Adam's transgression, man's curse, and the spiritual pandemic that infected all creation. Every pain man has ever experienced, every malady of evil that has ever touched him has its roots in chromosomal and spiritual Adam.

Egypt, biblically speaking, is synonymous with pain.

The first Egypt was not situated along the Nile River; it was created willfully and spiritually in the garden. This place of separation, isolation, and oppression was created when man swallowed the lie that he could determine good and evil for himself instead of letting God define it.

The historical Egypt and all the symbolic Egypts ever since require one common denominator for God's people: a condition of captivity that brings pain to self and others. So when I say that every man has his Egypt, I am saying that a believer has a former identity in the spiritual Egypt of their former world that was apart from Christ, held back and held down by their former partnerships with their culture, their sin nature, and the devil.

A nonbeliever, conscious or unconsciously, is in this spiritual Egypt, unable to experience God's love and plan for his life. The Pharaoh of this world and his axis of evil are still holding billions hostage, and he wants to keep them there (see my book *Fight*). He also is stubbornly chasing down believers by the millions, angry over being humiliated. He lures the delivered back to Egypt by playing on their insecurities and discontents. This is the real fight, the real ongoing story, and where the real work of the Holy Spirit *in* and *through* the man of God begins in powerful ways.

> *The Pharaoh of this world and his axis of evil are still holding billions hostage, and he wants to keep them there.*

It is called your deliverance.

Close to Home

The fight for your deliverance is the work of the Holy Spirit.

That initial and ongoing spiritual work of deliverance of God in our lives, like Israel's literal deliverance, is *the* shaping encounter for how we relate to God. More specifically, as we'll see, it forms the basis of the Spirit-formed, Spirit-filled, and Spirit-used life. Of little consequence to God is the nature of your personal deliverances. Of massive importance to God, however, is your perception of these experiences with Him that *set you free:* how those deliverances shape your own identity in Him and how the Holy Spirit seeks to use a delivered and filled man in the lives of others. As we'll see, when God goes to great lengths to deliver His people from any Egypt, He desires that they translate their deliverances into meaningful service for Him.

Moving God's people forward in their earthly mission is not a new dilemma. As a pastor, I am always seeking the best ways to get people off their "blessed assurance" and into their Spirit-appointed mission on earth. God's pioneering pastor, however, was Moses. He had to spiritually recalibrate his troops early and often. In fact, when he needed to light a fire beneath the feet of God's children, he had a tried and true formula to motivate, remind, and teach them about their purpose on earth. It was undeniably the strongest possible reminder of the character of their God and His love for them, and a simple way to think about their own purpose as God's chosen representatives on earth. Listen for the Holy Spirit's voice during one of these teachable moments with God's sons and daughters as Moses drops two pride-buster bombs designed to explode any idea of entitlement and create healthy doses of humility and openness to God's purposes for them.

> *When God goes to great lengths to deliver His people from any Egypt, He desires that they translate their deliverances into meaningful service for Him.*

The first truth-to-heart missile focused on their unique selection to be God's people. This fact, absorbed properly, produces a major attitude adjustment in anyone. How major? Trust me, when a man uses the metaphor of circumcision to get his point across, he's not playing nickel poker! *That* tone means business, and Moses certainly got the men squirming uncomfortably and paying attention. Listen in:

> To the LORD your God belong the heavens, even the highest heavens, the earth and everything in it. Yet the LORD set his affection on your forefathers and

loved them, and he chose you, their descendants, above all the nations, as it is today. Circumcise your hearts, therefore, and do not be stiff-necked any longer. (Deuteronomy 10:14–16)

The second laser-guided missile Moses deployed had a radically different payload and motivational force than the first. While the first bomb was factual, theological, and spiritual, this next doozie was rooted in something much more personal, much more meaningful, much more emotional, and central to the power of their relationship to God: *their deliverance.*

> For the LORD your God is God of gods and Lord of lords, the great God, mighty and awesome, who shows no partiality and accepts no bribes. He defends the cause of the fatherless and the widow, and loves the alien, giving him food and clothing. And you are to love those who are aliens, *for you your-selves were aliens in Egypt.* Fear the LORD your God and serve him. Hold fast to him and take your oaths in his name. He is your praise; he is your God, who performed for you those great and awesome wonders you saw with your own eyes. (Deuteronomy 10:17–21)

If there was any pride left after bomb number one, it's been incinerated with planned precision by bomb number two. Nothing like a good dose of reality regarding our hopeless condition, God's powerful intervention, and our salvation by His hand to set us straight! It worked then, it works now, and it will continue to work as the most effective antigen against pride and rebellion among God's creatures.

Why this focus on their deliverance? It is unshakably personal, highly emotional, vividly memorable, and deeply central to the relationship. These adrenaline-producing memories are undeniable, and they silence all resistance. It is from this emotional and spiritual story of deliverance that Moses guides them into renewed senses of God, self, and mission. Their deliverance gives them a new set of glasses through which to see their purpose on earth.

This was a "Come to Yahweh" moment.

God, through Moses, wanted there to be *no confusion* about

- His person and character.
- His interest in others.
- how His people should view themselves.
- who His people need to love.
- how His people make commitments.

Neither does the Holy Spirit want any confusion.

Our Deliverer

Deliverances (that is, our salvation and subsequent transformations) are designed by the Holy Spirit to change the way we view God, the way we perceive ourselves, the way we see others, and the way we go about representing God in the world. As we look to release the Holy Spirit's power in us outward to a waiting world, we must consider the nature of God's intervention in our own life if we are to confidently reach out to others in our blast zones of influence.

What must we see?

A Strong God Who Fights for Your Freedom

"For the LORD your God is God of gods and Lord of lords, the great God, mighty and awesome, who shows no partiality and accepts no bribes" (Deuteronomy 10:17). The Holy Spirit wants us always to have a right view of God, because without it, our accountability (fear of the Lord) and confidence in the mission ahead are shot. He wants us to get one thing straight: "*your* God" is unequaled, unparalleled, unmatched, and unimpeachable in strength and integrity. The fancier term for that is *strong*! We have been delivered by and brought into relationship with a mighty and awesome God who fights to set His people free. He is our warrior champion. This is also the family resemblance, and the Holy Spirit is tasked with reproducing His confidence in believing sons.

A Tender God Who Loves All Captives

"He defends the cause of the fatherless and the widow, and loves the alien, giving him food and clothing" (Deuteronomy 10:18). The Holy Spirit also wants us to bear this family resemblance of our God, the One who defends the vulnerable, those who are held captive by their circumstances and need a champion. Throughout Scripture we repeatedly see God's heart for the marginalized, traumatized, neglected, lonely,

> *Throughout Scripture we repeatedly see God's heart for the marginalized, traumatized, neglected, lonely, abused, and exploited.*

abused, and exploited. The common denominator is that these folks are disconnected and disenfranchised from the system because they don't fit the cultural norms. As a result they are desperately lonely in their circumstances, and God loves to meet their needs. In a culture that loves to make distinctions, to judge by appearance, and to give preferential treatment, this would be a big leap for God's people—if not for their own story of deliverance.

A Strong and Tender God Who Delivered This Alien

"For you yourselves were aliens in Egypt" (Deuteronomy 10:19). Captives know what it feels like to be held against their will by someone, something, or some circumstance beyond their control. According to the Bible, all Christians were captives, held hostage by sin, isolated from God, and consigned to spend eternity away from His presence. But then God spiritually delivered us out of this spiritual Egypt, not stopping with this one act but proceeding to deliver us from ourselves progressively to this day. The Holy Spirit has authored not only our salvation but every transformation of character and conduct as well. He defends us. He provides for us. He fills us. He secures our peace. He restores our worth.

A God Who Commissions Me to Deliver Aliens

"And you are to love those who are aliens" (Deuteronomy 10:19). Men become what they worship. If you love stuff, you become a materialist. If you love indulging yourself and worship feelings and thrills, you become a hedonist. If you love your image more than you love God and people, you become a narcissist. If you worship the "God of gods and Lord of lords" who defends the vulnerable, you become a tender warrior. This means taking on His character, conduct, and causes with aliens.

When Jesus charged the disciples saying, "Go make disciples," it was synonymous with saying, "Go fight for the captives," because freedom from sin and death through the Spirit would be the outcome. The Holy Spirit's mission in our lives is to conform us to the God we worship, and He is passionate about delivering people.

A God Who Wants Me to Make Commitments in Line with His Character

"Fear the LORD your God and serve him. Hold fast to him and take your oaths in his name. He is your praise; he is your God, who performed for you those great and awesome wonders you saw with your own eyes" (Deuteronomy 10:20–21). Through the Holy Spirit, God's Man shares God's heart. Making commitments in His name is synonymous with faithfully acting according to His character. Make no mistake: His character is to defend the vulnerable, the captive, the marginalized, the persecuted, the oppressed, the lonely, the left out, and the left behind. If we are listening to the Holy Spirit, our hands and feet will eventually take us toward the aliens among us. Aliens—as in people who are outside the borders of God's family but inside the domain of His people ready to be embraced, connected with, and adopted in the middle of their sojourn. It may take some time, some maturing, and some changes within us first, but eventually the Holy Spirit will raise us up as tender warriors who are unafraid and unapologetic to stand up for those who need a spiritual champion to fight for them.

The only question is this: Where is your field of battle?

The Heart of the Gospel

The heart of God is at the heart of the gospel.

In our discussion of the Holy Spirit, the axis for understanding our relationship and responsibility to Him in our world means to clearly see how our personal story of deliverance as believers is an expression of the heart of God. His movement toward us and for us is the exact picture of what should be our movement toward others in His name. When we see our own deliverance clearly, we

- see God more clearly.
- perceive our own condition and character more clearly.
- grasp Christ's mission on earth more meaningfully.
- understand the work of the Holy Spirit through us more fully.
- realize the goals of our ministry more fruitfully.
- identify with those we are called to reach more readily.
- identify with Christ as tender warrior more visibly.

Jesus defined for us how the heart of God would be at the heart of the gospel when He announced how the kingdom would roll out:

> "The Spirit of the Lord is on me,
>> because he has anointed me
>> to preach good news to the poor.
> He has sent me to proclaim freedom for the prisoners
>> and recovery of sight for the blind,
> to release the oppressed,
>> to proclaim the year of the Lord's favor."

> Then he rolled up the scroll, gave it back to the attendant and sat down. The eyes of everyone in the synagogue were fastened on him, and he began saying to them, "Today this scripture is fulfilled in your hearing." (Luke 4:18–21)

Poor. Captive. Blind. Oppressed. These categories depict the *spiritual conditions* of the human spirit as well as the types of people whom Jesus sought to engage, deliver, and set free spiritually, physically, and emotionally. Poor, captive, blind, and oppressed portray the conditions of soul, frames of mind, levels of insight, and degrees of bondage the Holy Spirit is commissioned to fight against in order to bring liberty emotionally and spiritually. All require deliverance from their Egypts, their Pharaohs, and their slaveries. More practically, they define and describe the target audiences the Holy Spirit is zeroing in on—*using us!* These include all ages and races of people in all locations where Christ's tender warriors are deployed.

The poor of spirit become wealthy. The starving are fed and become full. The lonely are comforted and

> *Wherever you are, the Holy Spirit is. And wherever the Holy Spirit is, there is a mission to set people free.*

included. Those who have no perception of God now see Him clearly. The weary are relieved. In all ways and forms, Jesus continues to deliver the lonely, the left out, the left behind, and the marginalized, all of whom are in need of a champion. The Holy Spirit was upon Christ and now He is upon God's Man to accomplish these same anointed, ordained rescue missions on a global scale. Wherever you are, the Holy Spirit is. And wherever the Holy Spirit is, there is a mission to set people free.

> Now the Lord is the Spirit, and where the Spirit of the Lord is, there is freedom. And we, who with unveiled faces all reflect the Lord's glory, are being transformed into his likeness with ever-increasing glory, which comes from the Lord, who is the Spirit. (2 Corinthians 3:17–18)

The Holy Spirit makes men who are like Jesus—fearless, focused, and filled with God's power—to deliver freedom to waiting souls. We see the Holy Spirit taking up this mission at Pentecost, raising up 120 tender warriors ready to do His will and be delivered to their death if necessary. These men, under the influence of the Holy Spirit, show us exactly how to continue the expression of God's heart for spiritual captives. In these last chapters, we are going to see how the Holy Spirit wants to work through you to

- relieve someone's pain.
- reduce someone's load.
- raise someone's spirits.
- reach someone's soul.

Jesus said we would be His witnesses: men who give evidence after seeing, experiencing, and encountering the Holy Spirit that leads to further encounters with His delivering power. Men who, in His character, are ready to fight for the freedom of everyone who is held captive.

> *Jesus said we would be His witnesses: men who give evidence after seeing, experiencing, and encountering the Holy Spirit.*

It's time to run to the battle.

Holy Spirit, thank You for seeking me out and setting me free. I remember my deliverance. I remember my Egypts and the condition of my heart and soul without God. I remember the joy of my salvation and Your healing power in me over the years, changing me and giving me victory over my darkest sides. I reflect on the ongoing war for freedom within and around me, and I need Your power in my life for those fights. I need Your continued work of freedom and healing in my life. I praise You for being my strong and mighty deliverer.

Holy Spirit, I recognize Your desire to deliver and free people by using me as Your vessel. I accept. As Jesus fought for my spiritual freedom, I accept the mission of fighting for the freedom of others, with Your presence assuring me and anointing me for the work. Give me Your eyes for the alien, the poor, the blind, the captive, and the oppressed. As I see, help me to pray. As I pray, make me willing to speak up, lift up, show up, and stand up for the ones Jesus loves and died for. Help me to forget myself and my needs so that I can enter their lives and their need to know their deliverer and experience new freedom.

Make disciples through me. In Jesus's name. Amen.

relieve someone's pain

While women weep, as they do now, I'll fight; while children go hungry, as they do now, I'll fight; while men go to prison, in and out, in and out, as they do now, I'll fight; while there is a drunkard left, while there is a poor lost girl upon the streets, while there remains one dark soul without the light of God, I'll fight—I'll fight to the very end!

—WILLIAM BOOTH

In late November I sent a note to a friend: "Hey, Rick, my family is praying for a single mother with children we can encourage like we did last Christmas. Do any of your people know of someone who is struggling to make ends meet as a single mom?"

His reply: "Yes, I have just the person."

One month later my son and I were at a massive apartment complex. It was a rainy December night, and the temperature was unusually cold for Southern California. Our car was loaded down with colorful bags of wrapped presents, and there was something joyful and risky about what we were doing. We joked that we were on a "mission from God" to find our drop zone, deliver the packages, and rendezvous at "extraction point Charlie."

As we rolled down another street, I stared up through the windshield, squinting for clear lines of sight between the blurry and clear strokes of the wipers and looking for a building number. I mumbled to myself and God at the same time: "Come on, eighty-six… Where are you, baby? I need building number eighty-six. Lord, show me building eighty-six."

We had found the thirties and fifties section of the complex but were completely clueless of the housing numbers. Sensing another dead end, I put our truck in reverse again, mumbled some more, and turned down a different street, hoping to encounter some divine providence. On the new street the numbers on the building to the right read "No. 80," then "No. 82," and so on, until I pulled in front of building eighty-six. Alleluia! My answer to prayer felt a bit like dumb luck, but I was overjoyed and relieved.

"Okay, dude," I said to my son. "*You* are going to bring all this stuff to the door."

"Me? Why me?" he replied.

"'Cuz she might recognize me. But she has no clue who you are, and it's better that way. Apartment twenty-five is right through this courtyard. You can see it from here. Look…"

I don't think Ryan would have hesitated had it not been for a shady-looking character having a smoke in the rain outside the building. The man had a black hooded sweatshirt pulled over his head, and he looked menacing in the dark. He was positioned at the mouth of the courtyard, acting like a sentry. Ryan would have to walk by him to get to the apartment door, which I could see through the gap in the buildings.

Looking at Ryan I laid it out for him. "I am right here, watching you all the way. You have to do it. We don't have her phone number, and we can't leave the stuff on the porch in the rain. Besides, we have Darth Vader over there watching us, so we definitely can't ring the doorbell and run. I can see you the whole way. I am *right here.*"

"Okay. What do I say?"

I bit my lip for a few seconds, staring at the door with a gold-plated "25" on it, and thought about his question. With the truck engine running, the sounds of rain peppering the roof, and an ominous character taking another drag off his cigarette, our mission was at a turning point. Helping a thirteen-year-old talk to an adult and delivering a bunch of gifts anonymously—courteously and nonthreateningly—is not as easy as it seems.

"Okay, say this: 'Are you Terrie?' so you can confirm we have the right place. Then say, 'I have some gifts for you and your daughter.' Hand her the gifts and say, 'Merry Christmas.' That's all you need to do. Got it?"

Ryan nodded, got out of the truck, grabbed all the bags from the backseat, and was off to number twenty-five. He passed the bogeyman just fine, ambled through the rain across the courtyard, got to the green door, knocked on it, and waited. After about thirty seconds, I had a sinking feeling that no one would answer. Our intel had said this would be the best time to deliver. I watched Ryan knock again, and after about five seconds, the door opened. As Ryan quizzed the short Asian woman in the doorway, she looked a little perplexed. Her nod confirmed we had the right contact for Operation Solo Mama. Then I saw the woman look down quickly at her left leg, where a three-year-old in footed pajamas clung to her pants, curious about the large boy holding some packages.

Unable to hear any dialogue, I saw Terrie shrug her shoulders, clasp her hands over her chest, and engulf my son in what I know for him was an *uncomfortably long* bear hug. That's when, for me, time slowed and the moment hung in the air. For me, as a dad, the image of my son and this single mom on the porch in the rain is one for the ages. I got to savor it for all of four seconds before Ryan was released from the death grip. He gave his parting wishes for a merry Christmas and started running to his extraction point. When he jumped back into the truck, he was all smiles, his face flushed red, and his breath was visible from the cold.

"So, how did it go?"

"I told her I was just the delivery person and that the gifts were from a family at church. Then she hugged me."

"I saw that. Perfect, bro. Great job. Let's roll."

Mission accomplished.

For the entire year leading up to this cold December night, each family member had saved pennies, nickels, dimes, and quarters for the purpose of helping someone we would never know. But no one talked about it. The days passed, and leftover change steadily accumulated in jelly jars, mugs, jewelry boxes, and car ashtrays.

A few days before delivery day, the family spent an afternoon consolidating all the change, separating, counting, and making rolls of quarters, dimes, nickels, and pennies. Each year we have a contest to see who can guess the total amount, and then we look forward to learning the total we can put toward a family. We think through the practical and personal needs of a single mom and plot an attack plan for hitting different stores, getting gift cards, and selecting presents. We shop, wrap, pray, and deliver. And while there are many missions we participate in throughout the year, this one is special. It's entirely ours—from start to finish—as a family.

> *The Mighty One needs His mighty men globally, filled with His Spirit, to be mindful of those around them, doing His work, and creating anthems of praise on earth.*

The rush we all feel is simply knowing that whoever God selects for us will be someone who feels alone in her circumstance. We can come alongside her in Jesus's name. We cannot know what life would be like as a single working mother, but that night we rejoice that she is comforted and encouraged by God.

The hug my son received was worship. The smile on his face was worship. The joy we all experienced on Christmas morning was worship. The renewed hope was worship. When God remembers us tangibly, we feel more secure, less burdened, and more encouraged to face the realities before us. It is the mind-blowing realization that the God of the universe cares about our life, moves visibly toward us, and blesses us. Just like how Mary praised God when she told Elizabeth the good news of the coming of the Lord:

> My soul glorifies the Lord
>> and my spirit rejoices in God my Savior,
> for he has been mindful
>> of the humble state of his servants.
> From now on all generations will call me blessed,
>> for the Mighty One has done great things for me—
>> holy is his name. (Luke 1:46–49)

The Mighty One needs His mighty men globally, filled with His Spirit, to be mindful of those around them, doing His work, and creating anthems of praise on earth.

Showing Up

The Holy Spirit in a man brings help to others through that man.

Jesus used the word *Helper* four times in one discussion with His disciples to describe the nature and work of the Holy Spirit (John 14:16, 26; 15:26; 16:7, ESV). The Greek word is *paraclete,* and at its root are the concepts of advising, exhorting, comforting, strengthening, intervening, and encouraging.

When Jesus spoke to His men about the Helper, He knew the disciples would soon meet with great distresses, trials, difficulties, and persecutions. They would need all of the assistance that the Helper could offer to stay loyal, faithful, and productive in the midst of the greatest changes and challenges in their lives. *On the flip side,* filled with the Spirit's mighty presence and power, they would become agents of that same help, comfort, and encouragement, *producing healing and hope in the lives of others.* The disciples would accomplish this by *showing up* and *speaking up* in the lives of the people they would encounter.

This is the same mission the Holy Spirit seeks to carry forward in every disciple.

Our little family Christmas tradition is a good reminder to me that while big opportunities to help others rarely come, the small ones surround me daily. In baseball, they call it winning by "small ball," which is the strategy of steadily advancing base runners versus relying on the big home-run hitters.

As we seek to witness and give evidence of our relationship to Christ through the power of the Holy Spirit, let's look simply and closely at the character and conduct of Christ as well as the men of Pentecost. Both provide solid pictures of Spirit-filled men involved in the lives of others. By observing their living examples, we can aggressively cooperate with the Holy Spirit to *stand up* for the weak, *show up* to help others, *lift up* our brothers and sisters, and *speak up* for Christ before those He died to save.

In the process, we are going to become fruitful in the same four areas where the Holy Spirit is carrying out His work in us:

- Making us feel more secure in Christ
- Making us feel more supported by Christ
- Making us feel more strengthened in our walk with Christ
- Making us feel more steadfast in our witness for Christ

Since these represent the efforts of the Holy Spirit in us, they should also be solidly reflected in our expression of ministry toward others. The Holy Spirit is a *validating force* in the life of the believer, providing assurance that God's presence and purpose in our lives are real and tangible.

Let's look at each expression going outward from Christ and from the men of Pentecost to define some simple ways the Holy Spirit is calling us to validate God's presence and purpose in the lives of others.

Make Secure

He loved the ragamuffins.

The Holy Spirit moved upon Jesus regularly to stand up for the vulnerable, stigmatized, and isolated to make them feel accepted by God, secure in His presence, and affirmed as people worthy of salvation. The ethnically, morally, physically, and culturally unacceptable were all deemed acceptable by His simple presence among them. For these segments of the population, spiritual types were not easy to be around. Yet these same outsiders were completely at ease around Jesus.

Lepers, prostitutes, Samaritans, tax collectors, gluttons, children, women, the diseased, crippled, mentally unstable, and all garden-variety sinners were at home with Jesus *because of the Spirit of the Lord that was upon Him.* In fact, the knock on Jesus was that His standards were very low when it came to His associations and locations of ministry. But by working seamlessly with the Holy Spirit, Jesus fully expressed the heart of God toward these aliens in His own culture, challenging the disciples at many levels and, on more than one occasion, causing reactions among them.

> *Lepers, prostitutes, Samaritans, tax collectors, gluttons, children, women, the diseased, crippled, mentally unstable, and all garden-variety sinners were at home with Jesus* because of the Spirit of the Lord that was upon Him.

Father, Son, and Holy Spirit were drawn to these souls because of how their spirits had been crushed, their dignity robbed, and their future stolen by their culture or circumstances. So God in the flesh made it His mission to restore *all three* back to them by His presence and help. He called them the "poor in spirit," the "blind," and the "sick" who needed a physician to restore wealth, insight, and health spiritually. The richest encounters for Jesus were with those who were poorest in spirit, flipping both religious and male cultures on their head.

The men of Pentecost followed suit in the Spirit. Fresh from the upper room, they ran head-on into cultural and religious discrimination against certain widows who were falling through the cracks in the system. It could have easily been glossed over in the chaos of the moment, but the Holy Spirit would not allow it. Instead, men full of the Holy Spirit mobilized to make those who felt forgotten secure.

Watch the film and, more specifically, see the results of the mobilization to minister to widows.

> But as the believers rapidly multiplied, there were rumblings of discontent. The Greek-speaking believers complained about the Hebrew-speaking believers, saying that their widows were being discriminated against in the daily distribution of food.
>
> So the Twelve called a meeting of all the believers. They said, "We apostles should spend our time teaching the word of God, not running a food program. And so, brothers, select seven men who are well respected and are full of the Spirit and wisdom. We will give them this responsibility. Then we apostles can spend our time in prayer and teaching the word."
>
> Everyone liked this idea, and they chose the following: Stephen (a man full of faith and the Holy Spirit), Philip, Procorus, Nicanor, Timon, Parmenas, and Nicolas of Antioch (an earlier convert to the Jewish faith). These seven were presented to the apostles, who prayed for them as they laid their hands on them.
>
> So God's message continued to spread. The number of believers greatly increased in Jerusalem, and many of the Jewish priests were converted, too. (Acts 6:1–7, NLT)

Widows and victims of discrimination, meet your new best friends: *men full of the Holy Spirit. KUH-BOOM!* Cultural barriers crumbled, the vulnerable were not victimized, the onlookers were blown away, and hearts melted.

> *A witness started building. Male culture started acting out of character. And stuff started happening. That is the story of the men of Pentecost.*

Then a fresh wave of the Holy Spirit took over the streets and synagogues, resulting in yet another explosion of growth. All of this because people who were being left out were now intentionally included and cared for. The Holy Spirit was saying: "Make them secure. Don't forget them because of racial or other issues. Give them your best men and best efforts and watch what happens!"

The message: Include everybody!

When you look at the ministry of Jesus and the men of Pentecost, you see walls falling down: ethnic walls, cultural walls, economic walls, and even religious walls. You can't miss this! The Holy Spirit was at work, transcending the established culture to make the most vulnerable among them feel secure. In the process, everyone present was witness to the authority of the kingdom of God over the cultures of men. A higher allegiance was seen. A witness started building. Male culture started acting out of character. And stuff started happening. That is the story of the men of Pentecost.

This is your story as well.

It is a hard-fought place to reach, but the Scriptures tell every God's Man he must find a higher law that allows

> **soar fact**
> *The Holy Spirit wants to demonstrate that God's Man operates under a higher law, a royal one that gives him freedom to cross all cultural lines to make sure people feel included.*

him to enter freely into the lives of people without hesitation. Listen up to your brother James putting the screws to those who act culturally and practice selective sympathy:

> If you really keep the royal law found in Scripture, "Love your neighbor as yourself," you are doing right. But if you show favoritism, you sin and are convicted by the law as lawbreakers. For whoever keeps the whole law and yet stumbles at just one point is guilty of breaking all of it. For he who said, "Do not commit adultery," also said, "Do not murder." If you do not commit adultery but do commit murder, you have become a lawbreaker.
>
> Speak and act as those who are going to be judged by the law that gives freedom, because judgment without mercy will be shown to anyone who has not been merciful. Mercy triumphs over judgment! (James 2:8–13)

The Holy Spirit does not single out some and leave out others.

All of us have felt rejected. The Holy Spirit hates that feeling as much as we do, and in God's family there are no cousins or in-laws—only sons and daughters. The opportunity to go from a creation of God to a child of God is available to all. Men made strong by the Spirit provide an equally strong sense of comfort for the captives by treating them like family, whether or not they are members yet. Here's how.

1. God's Man makes others feel secure through inclusion.

> And *you also were included in Christ when you heard the word of truth,* the gospel of your salvation. Having believed, you were marked in him with a seal, the promised Holy Spirit, who is a deposit guaranteeing our inheritance until the redemption of those who are God's possession—to the praise of his glory. (Ephesians 1:13–14)

Translation: There was a time when you and I were not first family. God let us in, the Holy Spirit signed for us and marked us for first-class delivery to heaven. We didn't earn it or deserve it. Such a man, accepted graciously by God, should be the most accepting and inclusive man on the planet. God wants us to remember that the kingdom of God is open for business to all who come in contact with it. This is especially true for those who have been made to feel less than worthy or left out of God's plan in any way.

2. God's Man makes others feel secure through protection.

> Pure and genuine religion in the sight of God the Father means caring for orphans and widows in their distress and refusing to let the world corrupt you. (James 1:27, NLT)

Translation: Men can act according to their culture's values or according to the values of the Holy Spirit in the character of Christ. A tender warrior looks after those in his context who are unable to defend themselves or are vulnerable. The men of the church are the sleeping giant who can, if united, turn the tide of the world's worst exploitations of women and children. But they must stand up as one for the vulnerable. This is Christ, this is a man of Pentecost, and this is a God's Man full of the Holy Spirit. We look after the vulnerable ones to prove our faith and say no to the culture's exploitation, apathy, and neglect.

3. God's Man makes others feel secure through provision.

This is how we know what love is: Jesus Christ laid down his life for us. And *we ought to lay down our lives* for our brothers. If anyone has material possessions and sees his brother in need but has no pity on him, how can the love of God be in him? Dear children, *let us not love with words or tongue but with actions* and in truth. (1 John 3:16–18)

Translation: Sympathy is not a substitute for action. The Holy Spirit at work in Jesus loved sacrificially and heroically in order to provide for our salvation and transformation. He provided His body and blood to make us secure in our salvation. The Holy Spirit will call upon all God's Men to sacrifice of themselves materially to make others feel the peace and security of being provided for by God.

4. God's Man makes others feel secure through direction.

"If any one of you is without sin, let him be the first to throw a stone at her." Again he stooped down and wrote on the ground. At this, those who heard began to go away one at a time, the older ones first, until only Jesus was left, with the woman still standing there. Jesus straightened up and asked her, "Woman, where are they? Has no one condemned you?" "No one, sir," she said. "Then neither do I condemn you," Jesus declared. *"Go now and leave your life of sin."* (John 8:7–11)

Translation: Jesus directed the would-be judge and jury of the adulteress to take a long, hard stare in the mirror, and in doing so, He made her feel more safe and secure. But He didn't stop there. He also directed the adulteress away from what created the most pain and insecurity—a life of sin.

So what direction will your actions in the Spirit take?

God's Man helps captives to feel secure. This is how Jesus operated, and this is where the Holy Spirit wants to create some meaningful collateral damage emanating out of your faith. But first, we must heed the scripture's warning about selective sympathy, take a strong look in the mirror, and define what an authentic faith really looks like. Jesus and the men of Pentecost suggest that authentic faith means submission to a higher law that gives us freedom to enter into the lives of others our culture would tell us to avoid.

It's time to start crossing the battle line.

Holy Spirit, I accept Your mission to the vulnerable ones in my world. Today, make me a champion to someone who is feeling forgotten by people or even by You today. Bring somebody to my mind right now or across my path that I can come alongside to be Your strong hands and feet. Forgive me for just being sympathetic toward the vulnerable and thinking that is adequate. Help me to lay down my life, sacrifice myself, and give of myself in order to restore someone's dignity and worth in Your name. That's what You did with me! Help me to remember that as I live.

Give me the courage and freedom, Holy Spirit, to cross all cultural lines that prevent Your love from flowing to those in need. Free me to live for an audience of one! Thank You, Holy Spirit, for helping me to feel secure in God's love, sensing His inclusion of me, His protection of me, His provision for me, and His direction to me out of His love. I am ready to let those same actions flow out of me toward others. Thank You for making me feel secure as a sinner. In Jesus's name I accept the mission in my world. Amen.

reduce someone's load

Do not let what you cannot do interfere with what you can do.
—JOHN WOODEN

"Did my calf muscle just snap?"

It felt like somebody had hit the back of my leg with a baseball bat.

I was back-pedaling on the football field, watching the developing play closely so I could make a break on the ball once it was airborne. When I saw the ball coming in my direction, I planted my right foot and tried to push off. That's when I heard an awful sound, felt an excruciating pain in my calf, and crumpled to the ground. It looked grotesque, and I feared the worst—not so much the physical consequences of my latest sports injury but the relational consequences my injury would incur with my wife.

Say what? It was the setup for a perfect husband-wife storm.

Back home, my family was in the middle of packing up our two-story home, and we were moving in six days. Chrissy was hard at work, packing and getting everything ready. As I left to play that day, she lovingly fired a prophetic warning across the bow of my conscience: "If you get injured playing football, I am going to kill you."

Her sixth sense had told my sweet wife that, with the move upon us, a potentially ruinous scenario might play out: Kenny physically *out of commission.*

Now you know why the physical pain was secondary to the emotional firestorm waiting for me back at Packing Central. This was not going to be a good week for me.

Chrissy's best and only mule was dead.

When it comes to marital stress, moving is right up there with money issues, job transfers, unwed teenage pregnancies, sexual dysfunction, the empty-nest syndrome, midlife crises, and menopause. Bad news like mine *during* a move magnifies that tension, especially when the moving company is *you.*

I can usually work around obstacles and come up with alternative solutions, but a ruptured tendon was like Alcatraz: *there is no way to escape from this island.* This time I could forget about using my quick-thinking resourcefulness, intellect, or emotional fortitude. A tendon doesn't care about any of that. This was made painfully clear the next day at the orthopedic office when the doctor told me I should have heeded Chrissy's warning ("Thanks a lot, Doc. And I'm paying for this? Can't a guy catch a break?").

The next several days intensified my predicament as Chrissy and my mother-in-law feverishly wrapped, boxed, taped, and organized our belongings for the move. I felt like they should put me in the Goodwill or giveaway pile. I wasn't just feeling useless to them; I *was* useless. Some of my friends tried to console me by saying that I had no control over what had happened and that I should just relax and go along for the ride. Easy for *them* to say, right?

After five days of hopping around, it was clear that I was not going to be able to carry anything. I needed help, but it was Friday, and we were moving the next day. Who would be able to come at such late notice? That's when my cell phone rang.

"Kenny, it's Darren. How're you doing?"

"Not so hot, dude," I replied and then explained my man pain.

"I don't know if I can come, but I'll see what I can do."

"Thanks, Darren."

At eight o'clock the next morning I heard the rumbling of a large truck growling loudly down our street. I limped from the house to the driveway in time to see a huge construction truck, with twenty guys in back, pull up to my house. These men looked like a platoon of fresh marines ready for duty. They jumped out, filed into my home, and started hauling out all the big stuff. Smiling behind the wheel was Saint Darren, the patron saint for desperate masculinity. I wanted to leap for joy, but a firm handshake and thank-you would have to do.

Chrissy's face was transfixed and her pupils dilated at the sight of all this muscle going to work for her and bailing me out. I have never been so happy to see a group of men in my life, and I have never felt so helpless yet so relieved at the same moment.

My load was being carried for me.

All these guys abandoned their Saturday plans when Darren put out the call, brought themselves, their tools, their trucks, and their big hearts to help their wounded leader move and resettle. They did in six hours what would have taken my wife and a few others two days. They installed the washer and dryer, put the beds together, placed all the furniture exactly where Chrissy wanted it, and did all of the heavy lifting.

> *These men went the* second mile *for me.*

Neither the Seventh Calvary, Patton's Third Army, the Eighty-second Airborne, nor the Spanish Armada looked more glorious than that flatbed full of God's Men rolling up my driveway that Saturday morning.

These men went the *second mile* for me.

Make Lighter

When Jesus was explaining to His disciples how they would really turn heads, He gave them a picture that did not compute. He engaged in what could best be described as rhetorical overstatement to make His followers look closely at their own values. It was *deliberate and obvious* exaggeration intentionally designed to challenge His followers, address an issue, and make a point. Listen in:

> You have heard that it was said, "Eye for eye, and tooth for tooth." But I tell you, Do not resist an evil person. If someone strikes you on the right cheek, turn to him the other also. And if someone wants to sue you and take your tunic, let him have your cloak as well. If someone forces you to go one mile, go with him two miles. Give to the one who asks you, and do not turn away from the one who wants to borrow from you. (Matthew 5:38–42)

Say what? If His listeners took what Jesus said literally, they were about to spend their lives being abused, codependent, naked, and broke! Jesus's words were clearly intended to strike at an issue central to His own life mission, the people He would die for, those who would choose to believe in Him, and the ongoing work of the Holy Spirit in and through Christians. The issue? *Human selfishness.* He used the same type of hyperbole and exaggeration as recorded in the gospel of Mark when He told people to gouge out their eyeballs and cut off their hands to get them to take sin seriously.

> *Look for opportunities to be unselfish. Leave the perceived injustices connected to your efforts in God's hands.*

His can't-miss application point in this uncomfortable but forceful exposé on human selfishness is this: Value others in consistent and concrete ways. Look for opportunities to be unselfish. Leave the perceived injustices connected to your efforts in God's hands. This is faith in action: trusting Him to use your unselfish and generous actions to show His love at work in your life. To be able to act unselfishly in the interest of another is truly a work of God in a believer's life. But to act unselfishly in the midst of an unfair, unjust, and oppressive situation is truly a witness to others of His divine power at work in us. How? Because they know us.

There's more to Jesus's second-mile reference than is readily apparent. At the time, the Roman army occupied Palestine, and because the government didn't pay for all of a soldier's provisions, the occupying soldiers could requisition whatever they needed from the conquered people. Roman soldiers were known to abuse the privilege, and this issue was a hot button for all Jews living under Roman rule. When asked, the residents of Judea would have to stop what they were doing, put their own agenda on hold, and carry a soldier's armor or pack for one mile. For every Jew listening to Jesus's words, going a *second mile* to serve an oppressor was unthinkable, traitorous, and out of the realm of natural response.

And that is exactly what Jesus knew they would be thinking, providing a perfect backdrop to contrast what His own life, kingdom service, and Holy Spirit living was all about: submitting to unjust demands and exceeding them for a higher purpose.

Jesus was emphatic: His followers could not move the kingdom of God forward without paying a personal price and serving others *extravagantly*. By doing the unexpected to make *someone else's* load lighter, the Jesus followers would capture attention and create a witness for the gospel.

Jesus modeled this "shock service" to His men when He served them as they ate, washed their feet, cooked them breakfast, and ultimately died for them on the cross. In the process, He didn't squash their desire for greatness; He simply redefined the meaning of courage:

> *By doing the unexpected to make someone else's load lighter, the Jesus followers would capture attention and create a witness for the gospel.*

Then they began to argue among themselves about who would be the greatest among them. Jesus told them, "In this world the kings and great men lord it over their people, yet they are called 'friends of the people.' But among you it will be different. Those who are the greatest among you should take the lowest rank, and the leader should be like a servant. Who is more important, the one who sits at the table or the one who serves? The one who sits at the table, of course. But not here! For I am among you as one who serves." (Luke 22:24–27, NLT)

The servant king?

The Holy Spirit warriors of Pentecost reproduced the greatness Jesus spoke of by sacrificing themselves for the sake of others. They boldly served the Lord by serving the people through selfless preaching, teaching, equipping, organizing, and reaching out.

> *The outpouring of the Holy Spirit upon the men of Pentecost was an unprecedented demonstration of service and ministry to people that resulted in the salvation of thousands.*

Under pressure and persecution, they lightened the load for others spiritually, physically, and materially—trusting God with whatever losses they would incur by going the second mile.

In the process, a massive audience watched and responded to the different behaviors on display with interest and engagement. Wave after wave of second milers were captured, released, and put back into the water stream to spawn new fruit.

The outpouring of the Holy Spirit upon the men of Pentecost was an unprecedented demonstration of service and ministry to people that resulted in the salvation of thousands.

All the believers devoted themselves to the apostles' teaching, and to fellowship, and to sharing in meals (including the Lord's Supper), and to prayer.

A deep sense of awe came over them all, and the apostles performed many miraculous signs and wonders. And all the believers met together in one place and shared everything they had. They sold their property and possessions and shared the money with those in need. They worshiped together at the Temple each day, met in homes for the Lord's Supper, and shared their meals with great joy and generosity—all the while praising God and enjoying the goodwill of all the people. And each day the Lord added to their fellowship those who were being saved. (Acts 2:42–47, NLT)

These first disciples were the same gorillas who just a few weeks earlier had jockeyed for power among themselves! Then it had been all about them, their titles in heaven, and who would sit closest to Jesus. What happened? The Cross and Pentecost happened. What three years of watching the Son of God could not accomplish in driving out the selfish impulse, the most courageous acts of service and power did. They watched Jesus go the second mile and relieve mankind of an eternal load of guilt and sin through His own sacrifice on the cross. They watched Jesus love in the midst of oppression. They watched Him not retaliate. They watched Him give up all claim to comfort. They watched Him pay the price to advance the relationship between God and man.

Now, on the other side of Jesus's sacrifice and His departure, and filled with insight and power, the men of Pentecost were on fire and ready to make similar sacrifices for others.

They were now carrying the load.

Lighter Is Better

Jesus wants to relieve people of their burdens.

> Then Jesus said, "Come to me, all of you who are weary and carry heavy burdens, and I will give you rest. Take my yoke upon you. Let me teach you, because I am humble and gentle at heart, and you will find rest for your souls. For my yoke is easy to bear, and the burden I give you is light." (Matthew 11:28–30, NLT)

The mission of the Holy Spirit in you is to make this unburdening by Jesus real *in your experience* with Him.

People filled with the Holy Spirit are called to abandon agendas, rights, insults, and resentments and are asked to drop everything when prompted by Him to lighten another's load. This is what Jesus did, as did the men of Pentecost. And it's what God's Man does today.

Spirit-filled men end up doing things they never imagined in order to create a witness of His work in and through them. In fact, lightening the load of others is so mission critical that the apostle Paul was told by the Holy Spirit to make it a command for every New Testament believer: "*Carry each other's burdens,* and in this way you will fulfill the law of Christ" (Galatians 6:2). The Holy Spirit will help you do this in the following ways:

1. God's Man makes others feel lighter through His presence.

> For when we came into Macedonia, this body of ours had no rest, but we were harassed at every turn—conflicts on the outside, fears within. But God, who comforts the downcast, comforted us by the coming of Titus, and not only by his coming but also by the comfort you had given him. He told us about your longing for me, your deep sorrow, your ardent concern for me, so that my joy was greater than ever. (2 Corinthians 7:5–7)

Translation: Everyday life is heavy! Our very presence in the midst of a heavy season of pressure relieves and comforts people. Titus shows up, brings his infectious presence and perspective, and soon the others around him have gone from heavy and harassed to light and delighted. We carry one another's burdens by simply showing up to help. As we arrive and engage people, the pressure gets redistributed and sometimes even eliminated.

Someone did this for Titus, and now Titus, lighter and freer, is able to get out of his own head and show up for Paul. The Holy Spirit has others in your life right now who are needing your simple presence to help carry and reallocate the load they are under. Surprise somebody and show up in their lives and ask, "Are you doing okay? Let me help."

2. God's Man makes others feel lighter through providing what's missing.

> All the believers were one in heart and mind. No one claimed that any of his possessions was his own, but they shared everything they had. With great power the apostles continued to testify to the resurrection of the Lord Jesus, and much grace was upon them all. There were no needy persons among them. For from time to time those who owned lands or houses sold them, brought the money from the sales and put it at the apostles' feet, and it was distributed to anyone as he had need. (Acts 4:32–35)

Translation: Fill the hole! The Holy Spirit's best work through us is not fancy. When we see someone right in front of us, burdened by a particular need and we have the ability to help meet them, we simply ask, "What do you need?" Or we respond, and the help simply comes to their porch or mailbox. Big opportunities rarely come to us on a daily basis, but small ones are all around us.

When I overheard the huge audio-video guy in our building was only going to have an orange for his lunch the other day, the Holy Spirit said, *Kenny, go across the street, buy him a burrito, and fill his stomach.* I saluted, got it, came back, and plopped the food sack in front of him. His face was aghast. "Is this for me?" he asked.

That's the Holy Spirit filling a physical hole. Sometimes you will fill an emotional or spiritual hole. When you do, you lighten another's load.

3. God's Man makes others feel lighter by identifying with and presenting their needs to God through prayer.

> And pray in the Spirit on all occasions with all kinds of prayers and requests. With this in mind, be alert and always keep on praying for all the saints. (Ephesians 6:18)

Translation: I may not be able to take on or take over many of the burdens I come in contact with, but I know someone who *can*. Coming alongside and then coming underneath a heavy load many times outstrips our abilities, skills, and resources. But the Holy Spirit is ready to take on any need and bring it straight to the Lord. We don't need to hesitate to bring God's power and peace into a heavy situation through prayer. In fact, transferring burdens to the Lord is the lifestyle the Holy Spirit wants to build in our life as He lifts our burdens through prayer and as we help lift the burdens of others through prayer.

> *As we help people turn over their needs and burdens to the Lord, the Holy Spirit lightens their emotional overload and replaces it with increasing levels of peace.*

When we come into contact with needs *we can't meet*, we take them to God with that person. The result? They will feel lighter as someone takes over the responsibility for meeting their need: "Do not be anxious about anything, but in everything, by prayer and petition, with thanksgiving, present your requests to God. And the peace of God, which transcends all understanding, will guard your hearts and your minds in Christ Jesus" (Philippians 4:6–7). As we help people turn over their needs and burdens to the Lord, the Holy Spirit lightens their emotional overload and replaces it with increasing levels of peace.

4. God's Man makes others feel lighter through providing insight.

> Oil and perfume make the heart glad, so a man's counsel is sweet to his friend. (Proverbs 27:9, NASB)

Translation: When we are in the midst of pressure and heavy circumstances, our ability to think clearly and see solutions is almost always clouded. The problem is that we are too involved emotionally to think simply and rationally. We think things are fatal and final, or we wrongly assume everything's going to be okay, because then we don't have to accept responsibility for dealing with anything. In both cases, what we need is someone who doesn't have an agenda or a conflict of interest, who can come alongside, assess the situation, and offer a solution.

Many times a simple solution eludes me because I'm too caught up emotionally in the problem. But then a good friend of mine, Paul, will come along and offer me his unpolluted insight, and my eight-hundred-pound gorilla turns back into a hamster-sized problem. Sometimes the insight makes me feel sensational, and at other times it

> *The second mile costs us our selfishness, but it gains us a witness.*

demands obedience. In either case, my heavy load gets lighter through godly insight. "The right word at the right time is like a custom-made piece of jewelry, and a wise friend's timely reprimand is like a gold ring slipped on your finger" (Proverbs 25:11–12, MSG).

The Holy Spirit's words and insight through you to someone else will be very practical in nature and create real solutions that honor both God and people.

God's Man shows up in the lives of others ready to do the unexpected, to go the second mile, and to pay a price so that burdens can be lifted. The second mile costs us our selfishness, but it gains us a witness.

A Holy Spirit Warning to Men

There is no such thing as second-mile service without meeting our first-mile responsibilities. I see guys all the time trying to pole-vault over first-mile responsibilities in their marriage and with their kids while doing a bunch of service related to ministry or projects *outside the home front.* That kills their witness for Christ. It's what the Bible calls "dead works." A man is running around and helping others while his ministry at home is MIA with the wife and kids. These guys won't lift a finger to lighten the load around the house or with family members, but they will offer their best energies and efforts to help total strangers.

God's Man, remember this: Your first mile is where you meet the responsibilities already in front of you. The second mile is your *free choice to lighten someone else's load.* If you are not married, the same advice can be applied to honoring your parents, your close friends, or your spiritual family. First-mile work *first.*

Being a responsible first miler will cost you something, but it also will gain you integrity in your second-mile witness.

> *Holy Spirit, thank You for helping me to feel unburdened spiritually by Jesus. It feels amazing to know that my personal load of guilt and sin has been lifted by Him and replaced with a feathery blanket of forgiveness and hope. There are no words that properly express my gratitude. Thank You for continuing to carry and lighten my burdens in my fight with sin, to ease my struggle to make sense of circumstances, and to reduce my anxieties over the future.*
>
> *I accept the mission to do the same in the lives of others. Help me to clearly see the borders of where my abilities end and Yours begin. Help me to see the simple ways I can be used to alleviate the heavy loads people are carrying by providing what's missing, supplying insight, affording opportunities to pray, or simply making myself available. You are the one who does all the heavy lifting, Lord. I am Your servant. Help me to start lightening the load in my own first-mile responsibilities and then move me to the second mile for people I can help.*
>
> *I pray for the burdened around me in Jesus's powerful name. Amen.*

raise someone's spirit

The really great man is the man who makes every man feel great.
—G. K. CHESTERTON

Leaders are lonely.

That is why I like to speak to them as an outside hitter. I am not on their payroll, not beholden, not a groupie, not on their board, not a critic, not a family member, not a shareholder, and not paying a personal price for their performance, good or bad. I have no agenda, no attachments, and no preconceived notions about them.

Yet having said all that, I do know a lot about them. For starters, I know that most of the time the people under them say what they want them to hear, not what they need to hear, because of conflicts of interest, position, power, or the pedestal effect.

I also know that being *in command* at work makes the transition to the home front difficult for many men, because wives and kids don't care about their achievements, titles, expertise, or productivity, or that Daddy landed a huge contract. They just want a husband or a dad who gives them his time, love, and heart.

I also know leaders who are at war to keep the job, career, or professional demands from killing their precious and private sources of intimacy and connection (that is, their marriage and their family). Many lose this battle in the end—more than half to be exact.

Read on, leader man.

I know leaders take on pressures that are subconscious, subtle, and strong that, over time, create emotional fatigue. I know they get critiqued and criticized in private conversations by the people who are close to them. But those same people sit with them regularly, lips zipped, unwilling to say what's on their mind. I know leaders fail to meet the expectations of many, and while they know this goes with the territory, they still want to win as many of those people over as possible. I know people are counting on them to perform, open doors of opportunity for them, and navigate the future magically with their leader's edition crystal ball, ensuring that everything will be okay.

I know they have to make very hard decisions that impact people's futures, and these decisions are tough to set aside or compartmentalize. These decisions are theirs alone to make.

Got a fever now?

I know that leaders are truly loved and then loathed, sincerely appreciated and then attacked, and create both devotion and doubt, depending on their last success or failure. I know that their leadership style is analyzed, scrutinized, inspected, dissected, and often disparaged. I know that both their successes and failures are used like a magnifying glass to uncover their flaws.

> *I know that leaders are truly loved and then loathed, sincerely appreciated and then attacked, and create both devotion and doubt, depending on their last success or failure.*

I know that they deeply care about the *trust of their responsibility,* suffering many restless nights as they reflect on strategy, people, plans, the future, and how their performance will impact all of them.

I know that on many days they long for a simpler life with less pressure, fewer eyes watching, more time for relationships, fewer interruptions, and fewer demands on their character. It makes fantasy or escapism very tempting at times. The emotional tax can become too much, and they take the bait of Satan, bite down on the hook, and have to live a public and secret existence simultaneously.

All leaders battle these issues.

It doesn't matter if you are a married father of three, a coach, a facilities manager, a sheriff, a pastor, a sales manager, or the CEO of a Fortune 100 company; this is what leadership feels like, whether you understand the dynamics or not. These are the bricks in our backpacks, the stresses and strains of being a man, the weights we alone shoulder, and the forces in play that make waking up every day a pleasure and a pain. This pressurization of life builds up and eventually gets relieved some way.

The media have a field day with how men relieve their stress. Ask the marketing team that came up with the "What Happens in Vegas Stays in Vegas" ad campaign. It's the model for how the world says to deal with the isolating pressures of leadership. The offer is direct: escape it, medicate it with some other feeling, and then go back to your life, business as usual. Press "Repeat" as often as needed. That's one way.

Or you can *distribute the pressure* by having a strong relationship with God and with others, *make use of the pressure* to grow yourself in these relationships, and enjoy regret-free downtime. This model of dealing with the pressures of life keeps more

> *We yearn for it like a Labrador pines for someone to toss him a tennis ball. We need it in our soul like our lungs need oxygen. We want it so bad but fail to put our finger on it most days.*

money in your wallet, your wife and kids loving you, and your body and mind free of headaches, hangovers, and holdover memories that pollute your life with guilt.

The Holy Spirit has given us all the right tools to deal with pressure and the spiritual armor necessary to defend against a relentless enemy who constantly messages us that taking a walk on the wild side will not hurt anybody (read *Fight*). One of the most powerful weapons in this battle that reduces pressure, dampens the power of temptation, and produces spiritual endurance is something that others often fail to give us in the midst of our struggle. Every man craves it, but he gets very little of it. We thirst for it like a parched man on a hot Texas day. We yearn for it like a Labrador pines for someone to toss him a tennis ball. We need it in our soul like our lungs need oxygen. We want it so bad but fail to put our finger on it most days.

It's called encouragement.

Publisher Robert Collier nailed it, not just for men, but for every human being on the planet when he observed this simple fact: "Most of us, swimming against the tides of trouble the world knows nothing about, need only a bit of praise or encouragement and we will make the goal."

I know exactly what he means, and I'm pretty sure you do too!

I *Never* Knew

"Pick you up in five minutes and we'll go over to Souplantation."

"Okay," Lance said over his cell. "I'll be outside the building."

My friend Lance and I met monthly as pastors in order to vent a little in a safe environment and check in as brothers. I always looked forward to these times because to me Lance was like Yoda from *Star Wars,* and I was the young Padawan apprentice, gleaning in the fields of his counsel. His feedback and throwaway comments were so good that sometimes I came out of a lunch with two pages of notes! He never had an agenda and neither did I.

We would just show up and start dialoguing over what projects we were working on, messages we were preaching, family stuff, theology, fathering, and the future, all between bites of food and sips of iced tea. It was on the tail end of one of these lunches that Lance unintentionally dropped a bomb on me.

We were back in the church parking lot, sitting in my big Dodge, tying up our last topic of conversation. As I told him that I would follow up on some of the stuff we'd discussed, I expected Lance to say, "Great, Kenny. I'll talk to you soon," or "Cool, Kenny. Thanks for lunch," or "Next time it will be my treat," or something that would put a period at the end of this long run-on sentence we called lunch. Instead, Lance opted for a comma and released the following cruise missile, triangulated to hit me dead center in the heart: "Kenny, I don't know if anybody has told you this lately, but I just want you to know how much we appreciate all you are doing here at Saddleback with the men of the church. I know how much energy and effort you are putting in, so I just wanted to tell you thanks for all you do."

KUH-BOOM!

Suddenly I found my breathing interrupted and my eyes welling up. *What is happening to you, Kenny?* I thought. *Good Lord, man, pull yourself together!* In a split second, however, I realized that all my attempts to stop this flood of rising emotion were useless. Awkward! Lance was witnessing my little meltdown from a distance of exactly one foot! Did he think I was going to confess a moral failure, an adulterous affair, or a grievous mistake that I couldn't hold in any longer?

I couldn't look at him, which really made him think the worst. As I stared at the dashboard of my car I could feel the tears squeezing out of my eyes, making a soft tapping noise on my pants. *What on earth is happening to you, Luck? The only time you ever cry is during communion!*

Lance, thankfully, was completely silent and waited.

After wiping my nose with the back of my hand, I grabbed my shirt and dabbed my eyes a few times. I took in a massive lungful of air, then exhaled through pursed lips, my cheeks bulging. It's that noisy blowing out of a breath people do right before they confess or say something emotional. With my voice catching, I gave Lance my best interpretation of why his words had made me react this way.

"Wow, Lance. Sorry about this. I don't know exactly where this reaction is coming from, but I have a good idea. Your words caught me at a real interesting time. I have been asking myself lately if anyone really knows or cares about what I do. I have been at this church since 1989, so people assume I am doing fine. I needed someone to say something like that to me today. I guess the combination of where I'm at and what you said hit a nerve. You really caught me off guard at a time when I was questioning if I should continue pressing the fight. I guess I was a little starved for some encouragement. The feedback from the guys is great, but this is different, as you can see. Obviously. So thanks. Thanks a lot. It means a lot to me to know that."

The Holy Spirit was being the Holy Spirit through Lance just being Lance.

Sounds funny to say it that way, but it makes the most sense to me. God knew I needed some validating. He saw my mojo ebbing, my endurance waning, my confusion growing in the absence of some encouragement to keep fighting for the vision He had laid on my heart for the men of Saddleback and the world. So the Lord sent me Lance, a Spirit-filled man, as His messenger for the purpose of strengthening and steadying my feet in the midst of my doubts.

Looking back, I remember that moment like it was yesterday, because it was so catalytic in my fight to stick with the vision of Every Man Ministries. In many ways I believe I am still here today having been given the privilege of personally touching millions of men, in large part due to those two sentences uttered almost eight years ago.

By the way, that hypothetical leader I described at the beginning of this chapter? That was me.

Strengthen What Remains

The Holy Spirit is a strong voice of encouragement in the family of God.

As we push forward to learn exactly what the Holy Spirit wants to push out of us, we must again look to the character and expressions of the Father, Son, and Holy Spirit in the Scripture—as well as at the men of Pentecost—to get some insight into His ongoing ministry of encouragement through God's Man to other servants of the Lord.

The Father Encouraging the Son in His Person

> As soon as Jesus was baptized, he went up out of the water. At that moment heaven was opened, and he saw the Spirit of God descending like a dove and lighting on him. And a voice from heaven said, "This is my Son, whom I love; with him I am well pleased." (Matthew 3:16–17)

At this point in Jesus's life He'd not preached a single message, performed a single miracle, or healed a single person. There was no following, per se. This blast of encouragement was the pure love of a Father, and it was given unconditionally.

The timing was intentional, as Jesus was now about to begin the arduous journey to reveal Himself to the world, to navigate the final leg of His earthly mission, and to train the Twelve to complete it. It was important for the Father to let the Son know that He was loved and to give Jesus in His humanity the exact encouragement from divinity that every man needs and longs for. The Holy Spirit was active in this moment too, descending upon Jesus and "lighting on him."

How relevant this is to us as men, because encouragement lights us up, and the Holy Spirit is still doing this for God's servants through us.

How relevant this is to us as men, because encouragement lights us up, and the Holy Spirit is still doing this for God's servants through us. Even now, let the Holy Spirit affirm you as a son of God with these words from your heavenly Father.

The Father Encouraging the Son in the Midst of His Mission

> After six days Jesus took with him Peter, James and John the brother of James, and led them up a high mountain by themselves. There he was transfigured before them. His face shone like the sun, and his clothes became as white as the light. Just then there appeared before them Moses and Elijah, talking with Jesus.

Peter said to Jesus, "Lord, it is good for us to be here. If you wish, I will put up three shelters—one for you, one for Moses and one for Elijah."

While he was still speaking, a bright cloud enveloped them, and a voice from the cloud said, "This is my Son, whom I love; with him I am well pleased. Listen to him!"

When the disciples heard this, they fell facedown to the ground, terrified. But Jesus came and touched them. "Get up," he said. "Don't be afraid." (Matthew 17:1–7)

In contrast to Jesus's baptism, when virtually no ministry had taken place, this encouragement from the Father to the Son followed a vigorous investment of time, travel, teaching, preaching, healing, and training of the disciples. It's not a stretch at all to say that Jesus was probably physically and emotionally running on empty. Our best indicator that this was the case is that these words from the Father were spoken in the context of Jesus retreating with the disciples. This was His practice when He needed to refuel. This was the moment God chose to give Him another special moment of encouragement.

Two men, Moses and Elijah, in their time had been tasked with intense earthly assignments by God, and they were present as well. That was no accident! These guys knew all about stress. I would love to have heard *that* conversation! Imagine Moses talking about his audiences with Pharaoh or Elijah describing his confrontation with the prophets of Baal. Can you imagine the two of them patting Jesus on the back and encouraging Him to stay the course in spite of His feelings at the moment? This was an enclosed space, custom built to encourage the Son. While we don't know what was said, we can infer from the Father's encouraging and affirming words to His Son that the purpose that day was to encourage Jesus in His work. Once again, Jesus was literally lit up physically and emotionally by His Father, the Holy Spirit, and the third parties.

The Son and the Holy Spirit Encouraging the Family of God in the Midst of Its Mission

Wake up! Strengthen what remains and is about to die, for I have not found your deeds complete in the sight of my God. Remember, therefore, what you have received and heard; obey it, and repent. But if you do not wake up, I will come like a thief, and you will not know at what time I will come to you.

Yet you have a few people in Sardis who have not soiled their clothes. They will walk with me, dressed in white, for they are worthy. He who overcomes will, like them, be dressed in white. I will never blot out his name from the book of life, but will acknowledge his name before my Father and his angels. He who has an ear, let him hear what the Spirit says to the churches. (Revelation 3:2–6)

It's as if Jesus put His hand on the apostle John's shoulder and said, "I need to get some messages of encouragement to My followers. Take some notes!" What follows is a simple pattern of encouragement, equipping, and edification custom-designed for believers who are encountering different struggles. By this example we can learn from Jesus and the Holy Spirit how to encourage other believers. Here's the blueprint:

- Recognize and celebrate their expressions of commitment.
- Review the specific obstacles or issues they are facing.
- Reignite their passion to overcome the obstacles in their path.
- Remind them of the reward if they are faithful.
- Remind them to actively listen to the Holy Spirit.

The Men of Pentecost Were Sent Specifically to Encourage Believers

The Lord's hand was with them, and a great number of people believed and turned to the Lord.

News of this reached the ears of the church at Jerusalem, and they sent Barnabas to Antioch. When he arrived and saw the evidence of the grace of God, he was glad and encouraged them all to remain true to the Lord with all their hearts. He was a good man, full of the Holy Spirit and faith, and a great number of people were brought to the Lord. (Acts 11:21–24)

In the midst of fluid and challenging moments of faith for many converted Jews and Gentiles, *in-person* encouragement was crucial if these believers were to remain faithful to Jesus. We see even more specifically in the example of Barnabas that the Holy Spirit enables Christians to encourage other Christians. Through Barnabas, we see that real-time spiritual encouragement is to be genuinely joyful, planned, and on purpose. Like Barnabas, when we come into contact with other believers, a joy should pervade our spirit as well as a recognition that all believers are at war to hold on to their faith and fulfill their God-given purpose on earth. The special ministry of encouragement is needed to fight the good fight.

> *The special ministry of encouragement is needed to fight the good fight.*

Lastly, we see the Holy Spirit's ultimate goal for using us to encourage believers: faithfulness. This separates believer-to-believer encouragement from all other types of words offered to them. Your words move the one being encouraged to "remain true to the Lord."

If we don't allow the Holy Spirit to express encouragement through us to other believers, by default our lack of encouragement gives permission for evil to fill the void and work to destroy our brothers and sisters in the Lord. Encouragement is a spiritual weapon that believers use, standing back to back, to fight off unfaithfulness to God.

Listen to the Holy Spirit coursing through the pen of the author of Hebrews, seeing and feeling his urgency:

> See to it, brothers, that none of you has a sinful, unbelieving heart that turns away from the living God. But encourage one another daily, as long as it is called Today, so that none of you may be hardened by sin's deceitfulness. (Hebrews 3:12–13)

Get this: a war is raging to stop encouragement from flowing believer to believer. Satan is well aware of the reality that underencouraged believers fall away from their faith, fall back into sin, and free-fall into self-deception and unbelief.

The Holy Spirit knows that encouragement is the oxygen of every believer's life. Without it, our faith dies—slowly, miserably, angrily, unnecessarily. That is why He ardently implores us to *not* disparage, critique, analyze, overspiritualize, carp on, judge, or condemn other believers in His name. It is not a spiritual gift, calling, or discipline to demean or diminish anyone's faith; it is a sign of insecurity.

> *The Holy Spirit knows that encouragement is the oxygen of every believer's life.*

Our job is to encourage, strengthen, edify, build up, fortify, support, and give a needed boost to our brothers so that we "strengthen what remains" (Revelation 3:2). Listen to the Holy Spirit through the words of the apostle Paul as he pushes believers to engage in spiritual warfare through being good at conflict resolution and equally good in the ministry of encouragement: "Let us therefore make every effort to do what leads to peace and to mutual edification" (Romans 14:19). Every effort versus what? Every effort versus little effort, sparse effort, half effort, or no effort to keep conflicts to a minimum and encouragement running on maximum.

Every effort means *every* effort.

Explosive Encouragement

So here are some concrete ways that God's Man makes every effort to get into the jet stream of Holy Spirit encouragement.

The Holy Spirit Encourages Believers in Community

> And let us consider how we may spur one another on toward love and good deeds. Let us not give up meeting together, as some are in the habit of doing, but let us encourage one another—and all the more as you see the Day approaching. (Hebrews 10:24–25)

Get in a small group of believers that meets regularly in a home to open God's Word, asks good questions, talks honestly, and prays sincerely for one another. There is no such thing as Holy Spirit encouragement without being in community with other believers filled with the Holy Spirit! Consistently connect with other believers to both give and receive the encouragement He wants to pour out.

If you are not encouraged in your faith, find another group where the ministry of encouragement is present. Satan throws a lot of energy into making you apathetic or cynical about connecting with other believers, mainly because he knows that it will provide you with the support you need to put up a better fight against his schemes.

Fight for community!

The Holy Spirit uses our will and our words to encourage.

> Do not let any unwholesome talk come out of your mouths, but only what is helpful for building others up according to their needs, that it may benefit those who listen. (Ephesians 4:29)

By definition, unwholesome exchanges between believers involve tearing down versus building up. The Holy Spirit inside of a believer helps to deliver targeted and helpful words that impact the heart of other believers to fit their situation. Spirit-filled encouragement says no to unhelpful or self-serving comments in order to say yes to directed support.

This means listening well so we can encourage well. This means being okay with another believer's successes and blessings in the midst of our own failures or tough times, knowing that God is working all things toward His purpose, good and bad. It means overcoming jealousy, envy, conflicts, and personality differences through the healing work and security the Holy Spirit provides. This means being with people long enough to know their needs and struggles in order to target life-giving encouragement.

Fight for more encouraging words!

The Holy Spirit Uses Your Spiritual Gifts to Encourage Believers

> So it is with you. Since you are eager to have spiritual gifts, try to excel in gifts that build up the church....
>
> What then shall we say, brothers? When you come together, everyone has a hymn, or a word of instruction, a revelation, a tongue or an interpretation. All of these must be done for the strengthening of the church. (1 Corinthians 14:12, 26)

Versus what? For your own visibility? to salve your own insecurities? to establish your own spiritual superiority? The warning would not be stated if the misuse of spiritual gifts did not exist. The apostle Paul had seen so much pimping of God for personal visibility, notoriety, and public piety he wanted to vomit: "Have you been thinking all along that we have been defending ourselves to you? We have been speaking in the sight of God as those in Christ; and everything we do, dear friends, is for your strengthening" (2 Corinthians 12:19).

The Holy Spirit's gifting of a believer is *not for the individual,* and once the attachment to his gift is polluted by pride, the believer harms rather than helps the body of Christ. The Holy Spirit knows that a little knowledge is a dangerous thing, so He says to use the knowledge He gives us to build up others according to their needs—versus building ourselves up according to our own needs.

Fight for the strength of the body of Christ!

———

The Holy Spirit gives believers the exclusive authority to encourage other believers. No one else can provide this service to your brothers and sisters in Christ: "For even if I boast somewhat freely about the authority the Lord

soar fact
The Holy Spirit gives believers the exclusive authority to encourage other believers.

gave us for building you up rather than pulling you down, I will not be ashamed of it" (2 Corinthians 10:8).

In other words, a Christian is the Holy Spirit's only officially endorsed and sanctioned ambassador of encouragement to God's sons and daughters. He is looking for us to shoulder this responsibility personally, proudly, and powerfully to defeat discouragement and unfaithfulness in our spiritual family, just like my friend Lance did for me in the church parking lot. In a very real way, we are our brother's and sister's keeper, as measured by our willingness to be used to encourage them.

> *A Christian is the Holy Spirit's only officially endorsed and sanctioned ambassador of encouragement to God's sons and daughters.*

Find someone to encourage today.

Holy Spirit, thank You for reminding me that in our family we encourage each other. Thank You for modeling this in the Father and in the Son and in Your uplifting work through Your people. Help me to remember to use the gifts and skills that You have given me to encourage others. Help me to listen well so I can encourage and strengthen my brothers and sisters. Help me to make every effort not to compete with any Christian but to connect with all in order to encourage their faithfulness to You.

Heal the parts of me that cause me to withhold encouragement from others. Reveal the hurts and resentments, the wounds and insecurities that create jealousy, envy, division, and personality conflicts. Love me out of those immature places of character so that I can be free to encourage those around me, especially those who are followers of Jesus.

From this place of freedom and healing in Christ, I accept my commission to exercise Your authority to strengthen every believer I meet for his benefit versus my own. Thank You for this wonderful mission of giving encouragement to others. Fill me and use me to raise the spirit of my brothers and sisters, even as You have raised mine in Christ. For the sake of the body. Amen.

reach someone's soul

Every man is a missionary, now and forever, for good or for evil,
whether he intends or designs it or not. He may be a blot radiating his
dark influence outward to the very circumference of society, or he may
be a blessing spreading benediction over the length and breadth of the
world. But a blank he cannot be: there are no moral blanks; there are
no neutral characters.

—Thomas Chalmers

"Brian, you need to meet the Man."

Slicing through the confusing fat of his conversation with a longtime friend, my
brother Chris put the real issue on the table. He had spent the previous thirty minutes listening to a high school friend and former party buddy tell his story of hitting
bottom and deciding to get sober. For years my brother had wanted to have this conversation with Brian, but until now the pain in Brian's life was not great enough to
create an opening. In this moment, however, there was maximum openness in Brian
because a fresh wave of personal pain exceeded his fears and his pride.

Chris listened intently to the painful circumstances of his old friend's life, and in the
process, he reflected on the many moments the two formerly shared chasing skirts,
racing cars, and partying hard. Many of the memories he'd just as soon forget, but
there were others that made him smile. The irony of this call was that Chris used to

be Brian's "brotha from anotha motha." The fact that God would allow Chris to be the one Brian called for spiritual advice was implausible, impossible, and comedic! Sure, and while you are at it, ask Osama bin Laden for help with grief management strategies!

So when Brian called, Chris thought to himself, *But for Jesus. Thank You, Jesus.*

Brian droned on about how his relationships were fragmenting, his career was disintegrating, and his mind was bending to the point of breaking. Chris listened and reflected on the broken glass *his own* choices had made him crawl through, and he thought also of the hurt people left in his wake. It seemed so long ago that the evil combination of isolation from God and powerfully destructive appetites had enslaved him. Brian's story jogged his memory and reminded him exactly how far he had come because of "the Man" who came into his life at his own bottom. He remembered the day, the hour, the church, and especially the freedom he felt in that moment when the Holy Spirit invaded his life through Christ.

Brian turned a corner at about the twenty-sixth minute of the phone call and started to talk about how he'd come home to an empty house two weeks ago and found all trace of his beautiful wife and four kids missing. Closets emptied, drawers left pulled out, toothbrushes missing from their holders, the minivan space in the garage empty, and Jackie's wedding ring on the dresser, placed intentionally next to a short note in her familiar script. Brian was now officially alone.

Sitting on the floor in his youngest daughter's room, Brian read Jackie's note through a vodka-induced stupor. She said that she loved him, but she was done. Just three small words penned hastily on a large yellow Post-it, but their impact sat like a ton of bricks on his chest.

For Brian, that moment was the "aha!" that Jackie had not created through years of arguing about Brian's drinking. In his haze he remembered the faces of his children. What would he do without them? These painful realities and his unwillingness to have a father's suicide be his legacy for his kids shattered all his pride. He loved his family, but he didn't know what to do.

Brian had no other choice but to fight for his life, and the first step was to completely eliminate a very old mistress: alcohol. At minute twenty-nine of the phone call, Brian told Chris he had gone to his first two Alcoholics Anonymous meetings, and while they were horribly uncomfortable, he knew that was the point. He was utterly humiliated by his own actions, and he had no defense other than to accept responsibility.

This is when the conversation turned spiritual.

"This is a spiritual program, Chris," Brian offered. "They are talking about God 'as I understand Him,' and I don't even have an understanding to get started with that one. You were the first person I thought of calling. You have been down this path and seem to know how to do this.
What do I do?"

Chris's simple answer: "Brian, you need to meet the Man."

The Holy Spirit was on the job, a step ahead of Chris, and He knew the exact way for Chris to relay the next spiritual step for his friend in the midst of his pain and confusion. He simply needed an introduction to Christ, and my brother was going to help make it for him in a way that Brian would receive it.

Chris's simple answer: "Brian, you need to meet the Man."

Drawing the Net

The Holy Spirit is fighting for the souls of those around you.

To say that you have a strong relationship to the Holy Spirit and a weak commitment to reaching souls is fantasy. If He is forming Christ in us, then He is creating a tender warrior, ready to battle for the eternal future of those He has placed in our life and commissioned to reach for Him.

Here's what reaching someone's soul looks and feels like in the power of the Holy Spirit.

The Holy Spirit Will Move Us to Sacrifice for the Lost in the Character of Christ

> Suppose one of you has a hundred sheep and loses one of them. Does he not
> leave the ninety-nine in the open country and go after the lost sheep until he
> finds it? (Luke 15:4)

Evangelism is synonymous with inconvenience. You have to leave someone, something, or some preoccupation in order to make another person the focus of your
attention. You have to leave the emotional safety zone of acceptance for the risk-filled
world of possible rejection. You might be called to cross cultural, political, ethnic, or
personal boundaries to deliver the goods.

> *When Jesus talked about leaving the "open country" to go after a lost sheep, He meant leaving the flat ground for the hilly, the easy path for the hard, the safe plan for the unsafe.*

When Jesus talked about leaving the
"open country" to go after a lost
sheep, He meant leaving the flat
ground for the hilly, the easy path for
the hard, the safe plan for the unsafe.

Today, leaving the open country could take us to a closed country, where the gospel's
not been shared. It does not matter. Wherever the lost sheep are, the Holy Spirit will
be there through His men.

The Holy Spirit Will Use Our Conversations to Testify About Christ

> When the Counselor comes, whom I will send to you from the Father,
> the Spirit of truth who goes out from the Father, *he will testify about me.*
> *And you also must testify,* for you have been with me from the beginning.
> (John 15:26–27)

Cooperating with the Holy Spirit is synonymous with talking often about Jesus
Christ. And while many interactions we have throughout the day are incidental,
many others can be monumental if we are in close contact with the Holy Spirit.

Think of the people God is calling you to get closer to *within the flow of your life* so they will consider the claims of Christ. Jesus's point above is simple and challenging: *if a relationship is important to you, you talk about it.* The same is true of the good news. By its very nature it moves those who know it to share it with others.

The Holy Spirit wants us to know and make known the clear terms of the gospel.

> Let me now remind you, dear brothers and sisters, of the Good News I preached to you before. You welcomed it then, and you still stand firm in it. It is this Good News that saves you if you continue to believe the message I told you—unless, of course, you believed something that was never true in the first place.
>
> I passed on to you what was most important and what had also been passed on to me. Christ died for our sins, just as the Scriptures said. He was buried, and he was raised from the dead on the third day, just as the Scriptures said. He was seen by Peter and then by the Twelve. (1 Corinthians 15:1–5, NLT)

It amazes me how many committed Christians have not worked out for themselves exactly what they believe about Jesus to the point where they are comfortable sharing it with others. It starts with our own testimony and what we believed when we came to Christ—nailing that and then giving others the same message for them to trust. Ask yourself: What was the message that took root in my heart that allowed me to turn from my self and sin and embrace the person of Jesus Christ? What did the Holy Spirit clear up for me? Why did it make sense then and not before? Why was it so meaningful? What status changed between God and me? How did God arrange for my salvation? What did the death and resurrection of Jesus accomplish for me personally? How did the information about Jesus turn into an invitation?

> *The Holy Spirit wants us to know and make known the clear terms of the gospel.*

These are all questions the Holy Spirit has answered in your life and wants you to reflect back to others.

The Holy Spirit Charges Us with the Responsibility to Persuade Others to Consider Jesus Christ

> Because we understand our fearful responsibility to the Lord, *we work hard to persuade others.* God knows we are sincere, and I hope you know this, too. (2 Corinthians 5:11, NLT)

Our ability to do the job of God's Man on earth involves a clear understanding of our responsibility. The Holy Spirit impresses on us the importance of talking meaningfully and sincerely to others about Christ—and sticking with it! Working hard to persuade others means working hard to listen to them, working hard in praying for them, working hard at getting down a clear presentation of the gospel, and above all, taking risks to move them toward the person of Jesus Christ in the best way possible.

The Holy Spirit will impress upon non-Christians the authenticity of the gospel message.

> When he comes, *he will convict* the world of guilt in regard to sin and righteousness and judgment: in regard to sin, because men do not believe in me; in regard to righteousness, because I am going to the Father, where you can see me no longer; and in regard to judgment, because the prince of this world now stands condemned. (John 16:8–11)

The best news ever is that the Holy Spirit's job is to take what I say and make it sing! The Holy Spirit convicts a person. That means that His job (not ours) is to move non-Christians into an awareness of God, a consciousness of their need, and a clear understanding of what they have to do, which is to repent from self-sufficiency and come to God humbly and dependently. You and I can't do that!

When you think of the Holy Spirit in your life, you cannot divorce yourself from His desire to draw the net as He fishes for men by using your eyes, your mind, your lips, and your willingness to be used to bring people into a full fellowship with Jesus. He is eager, on the job, and good at convicting the heart, and He knows the absolute best way to bring the message home.

And if you have prayed and prayed for another person and are ready to throw in the towel—don't! Instead, be praying for the Holy Spirit to open that person's heart to God in His way and for you to be ready to help at the right time. If there is one thing I have learned in twenty-five years of ministry, it is that the Holy Spirit's methods of softening

> *The Holy Spirit's methods of softening and cracking open the human heart to receive the gospel are numerous, sometimes bizarre, and always just right.*

and cracking open the human heart to receive the gospel are numerous, sometimes bizarre, and always *just* right.

He opens the eyes of the heart.

Bizarre Perfection

The Holy Spirit is a creative opportunist.

The twists and turns of a missionary's story are still fresh in my mind. His story was far-out but true and documented. Follow it with me, putting yourself in his shoes, like I did.

Imagine spending a year in the jungles of New Guinea, painstakingly constructing the indigenous language of a tribe that's never seen a missionary. Your assignment: earn their acceptance, establish a friendly presence, learn the customs, learn to speak the language, and learn the terms, words, and expressions of the people so you can tell them the story of Jesus. It takes the better part of a year, thousands of interactive moments, and a quick pen and pad—but you are successful.

Now, the only thing left is the work. You have to merge the languages of the Bible and the native tongue, assign the right vocabulary words and terms, connect the story lines across the cultures, and deliver the gospel for the natives to either accept or reject in their own context. The work of translation is difficult, but you feel, after asking many questions about the accuracy of your translation, that the story of Jesus has converted well and will be understood by your tribe. It's time to ask the elders for a gathering to talk of the Creator and His plan for all men. Your request is granted, the moment arrives, and while nervous at first, you begin communicating the story of Jesus from the gospel of John by saying, "In the beginning was the voice of God."

Even you are surprised at how intrigued the people are with your story about Jesus upon hearing of Him for the first time. They are listening intently, reacting, and talking to one another as they hear of the different events surrounding the "Son of Creator" who has a funny name. They are dialed in and want to hear more about the miracle man who heals people and talks of His Father-Creator. You could not be more pleased with how the process is going.

> *A year of painstaking work for "Hail, Judas"?*

Over the next week, your journey through the gospel takes them from His arrival on earth, through the Sermon on the Mount and the parables, to the Garden of Gethsemane, right through His betrayal by Judas, His trial before the council, and His death and resurrection. Exhausted, relieved, and eager for a response, it is time for you to hear their reaction.

After the final storytelling gathering, the tribal elder says that the story of the Son of Creator was good and there is a part of the story they are particularly excited about. You cannot wait to hear about their positive connection to the gospel. "That is," he continues, "the excellent work of Judas in betraying the Son of Creator with a kiss of death and getting him to the men who would nail him to a cross." The man Judas, in their opinion, is the hero, and Jesus is the weak one for letting Himself be tricked by a skilled betrayer!

A year of painstaking work for "Hail, Judas"?

I listened with rapt attention as missionary Don Richardson (author of *Lords of the Earth*) described this true but heartbreaking story of the mission field. *Brutal, dude,* I thought. As it turned out, the Sawi tribe Richardson had befriended idealized violence through trickery!

As Don continued describing this culture of revenge, I thought his takeaway would be "faithfulness in the midst of fruitlessness" or a pep talk on endurance and "hanging in there" for the gospel, no matter what.

In other words, the Sawi would not be transformed by the gospel.

Thankfully, this was not the case. Don described how the Holy Spirit took *the very thing*—violence—that drove the Sawi away from Jesus and toward Judas and used it to bring them back to saving faith in Christ.

One day Don observed a Sawi child being taken to a rival tribe. He asked why one of their own babies was being forced to live among their enemies. The tribesman explained to Don that if a child was offered as a peace gift from one tribe to another, wars between those tribes would never be settled violently. The Holy Spirit pounced on this and was waiting to show Don the opening. Fortunately, our missionary's Holy Spirit radar was on.

Richardson pondered what he was observing:

- A son is offered by the chief of one tribe to another.
- As long as the child lives with the other tribe, disputes are settled without violence and a condition of peace prevails.
- The son replaces vengeance as the focus in the minds of the people toward one another.
- No true peace is possible without the gift of a peace child.

Then the Holy Spirit whacked Don over the head with this insight: a peace child…Jesus…making peace between man and God!

Richardson went back to his dwelling for the next few days and reframed the story of Jesus in the context of the peace child custom. When he re-presented the gospel to the Sawi, this time the tribesmen responded positively, realizing that the Father-Creator had but one Son and how Jesus was offered to man as a peace child. The whole tribe converted to Christianity from a violent brand of animism.

God made every man to live for eternity: "He has made everything beautiful in its time. *He has also set eternity in the hearts of men;* yet they cannot fathom what God has done from beginning to end" (Ecclesiastes 3:11).

Unfortunately, a bitter war rages to keep every man from living for eternity. God's Men—you and I—are called to take advantage of the opportunities given us by the Holy Spirit to make connections between the real-life issues and the gospel in the lives of the people we know and encounter. Then we diligently pray, asking the Holy Spirit to place in our mind the best way to deliver the gospel to their heart. The Holy Spirit prizes a passion for the lost, willing cooperation with Him, targeted conversation, and an accepting spirit. Scripture endorses a flexible approach, combined with an eagerness to seize the opportunities when they present themselves.

Pray diligently. Stay alert, with your eyes wide open in gratitude. Don't forget to pray for us, that God will open doors for telling the mystery of Christ, even while I'm locked up in this jail. Pray that every time I open my mouth I'll be able to make Christ plain as day to them.

Use your heads as you live and work among outsiders. Don't miss a trick. Make the most of every opportunity. Be gracious in your speech. The goal is to bring out the best in others in a conversation, not put them down, not cut them out. (Colossians 4:2–6, MSG)

The best way to be a witness and give evidence of the hope that is in you is to allow the Holy Spirit to provide you with the intel, the opportunity, the clarity, the relevancy, and the integrity of connection people deserve.

The same Holy Spirit who used the pain of my brother's friend Brian and the bizarre tribal custom of giving a precious baby away to live with an enemy tribe is the same Holy Spirit who knows exactly how best to pull the trigger with those He places around us. We simply need to *use our head* and remember that He is *way ahead of us.*

From Fear to Freedom

The Holy Spirit moves men from fear to freedom in sharing the good news, just as the men of Pentecost experienced firsthand:

> Then Peter, filled with the Holy Spirit, said to them, "Rulers and elders of our people, are we being questioned today because we've done a good deed for a crippled man? Do you want to know how he was healed? Let me clearly state to all of you and to all the people of Israel that he was healed by the powerful name of Jesus Christ the Nazarene, the man you crucified but whom God raised from the dead. For Jesus is the one referred to in the Scriptures, where it says,
>
> 'The stone that you builders rejected
> has now become the cornerstone.'
> There is salvation in no one else! God has given no other name under heaven by which we must be saved." (Acts 4:8–12, NLT)

Peter's journey from fright and fear to freedom and fearlessness is a testimony to what the Holy Spirit wants to do in all of us in our context. Filled with the Holy Spirit, Peter was no longer living for an audience of many but for an audience of one. This is witnessed by his total lack of concern for the opinions of those he was speaking with—the spiritual heavyweights of his day. The difference between Peter A (the one who was scared by a little girl into denying he knew Jesus three times) and Peter B is the Holy Spirit.

The difference? No fear. This is what Peter did:

1. He drew attention away from himself.
2. He pointed his audience to Christ.
3. He gave credit to God for the work they had seen.
4. He clearly addressed their actions.
5. He clearly stated the gospel.
6. He left no wiggle room.

Peter's next sermon to this group got him a flogging and an order from the local authorities not to speak in the name of Jesus. That, too, was met by a total lack of concern, as the influence of Peter and the men of Pentecost kept exploding from the center as they passed on their experiences with Jesus Christ and a clear expression of the gospel to others. Their no to sharing Jesus was translated as an emphatic "Yes!" Watch the film of their response:

> The apostles left the high council rejoicing that God had counted them worthy to suffer disgrace for the name of Jesus. And every day, in the Temple and from house to house, *they continued to teach and preach this message: "Jesus is the Messiah."* (Acts 5:41–42, NLT)

So much fear characterized these men prior to the coming of the Holy Spirit. And so much freedom and fearlessness epitomized them after His fresh wind was kindled in their souls.

So much fear characterized these men prior to the coming of the Holy Spirit. And so much freedom and fearlessness epitomized them after His fresh wind was kindled in their souls.

The good news about the good news is that the Holy Spirit is way ahead of us, working in the hearts and minds of those we are called to reach for Jesus. What's important for us to consider and reflect upon is that we are doing what only we can do so that the Holy Spirit can do what only He can do.

The apostle Paul, one of the best evangelists ever, passes along his secret to being used by the Holy Spirit to reach a soul:

> You'll remember, friends, that when I first came to you to let you in on God's master stroke, I didn't try to impress you with polished speeches and the latest philosophy. I deliberately kept it plain and simple: first Jesus and who he is; then Jesus and what he did—Jesus crucified.
>
> I was unsure of how to go about this, and felt totally inadequate—I was scared to death, if you want the truth of it—and so nothing I said could have impressed you or anyone else. But the Message came through anyway. God's Spirit and God's power did it, which made it clear that your life of faith is a response to God's power, not to some fancy mental or emotional footwork by me or anyone else. (1 Corinthians 2:1–4, MSG)

Do you see it?

The Holy Spirit's "less is more" approach to reaching souls is tried and true:

1. We take the initiative to go to others ("when I first came").
2. We intentionally keep our testimony and message simple ("Jesus and what he did").
3. We let the Holy Spirit take the loaves and fishes of our obedience and multiply them into salvation and transformation of others' lives ("God's Spirit and God's power did it").

Every man is a missionary who is making his mark on the world. No man is neutral. Relieving someone's pain, reducing someone's load, raising someone's spirit, and reaching someone's soul is how the Holy Spirit wants to help you make your mark for Jesus Christ while on earth.

In times of change and challenge there is a bountiful and *receptive* audience for these missions of the Spirit. That journey from fear to freedom in your personal mission for God on earth depends on one Person in your life: the Holy Spirit. Are you ready to accept His power and go?

Don't fight Him!

Our final prayer…

Holy Spirit, thank You for this journey of discovering who You are and how You desire a close and personal relationship with me. Help me to keep talking to You the way I have been over the course of this experience. I want to continue to sense Your presence in my life, Your work inside me, and Your power through me to impact my world.

I want to join Your process in people's lives. Help me to be an agent of Your power, an ambassador, a humble instrument to share with others my hope in You through the gospel. Give me Your glasses to see people the way You see them, precious ones needing to know and experience God's love. Lost ones needing to find their refuge in their Maker and Savior. Lonely ones who need to find hope again through having their past forgiven and purpose for living. Deceived ones who need to experience the truth, freedom, and healing of Your work deep within.

Use me. Open my heart. Open my emotions. Open my palms. Open my lips.

Until I die, and in Jesus's name I ask all of this. Amen.

study guide

This study guide is designed to be used *after* the designated chapters assigned to each session have been read. Whether you are studying *Soar* as an individual or as part of a group, the goal is to dive deeper, wrestle harder, and sense God's presence and affirmation through processing and praying about what you are learning.

Read the Chapters

Each session (except session 5) will cover two chapters of *Soar*. As you read them, journal, make notes, or highlight pages in the book that speak to, challenge, or apply to you personally. In your reading and reflection give yourself to the stories, insights, principles, scriptures, applications, and prayers so that when you come to the study guide section, you will be equipped to explore the questions.

Key Passage

Each session will have a Key Passage that connects to the chapters you have read. Groups should read the passage out loud, and if someone in the group has a different Bible translation, ask him to read it aloud so the group can get a bigger picture of the meaning of the passage. To drive the concept deeper, commit to memorizing the Key Passage for each session.

Introduction and General Feedback

After you have read the Key Passage, have someone read the brief introduction aloud to remind everyone of the focus of the discussion. The leader should then invite the group to share any questions, concerns, insights, comments, or aha's arising out of their personal readings and prayers connected to the chapters. This will lead naturally into the questions.

Go Through the Questions

The questions are designed to focus on how each person relates to the main topics of the chapters. Remember, the questions are to serve the group and facilitate dialogue, not to elicit a particular answer. With that in mind, don't race through the questions. Take your time and allow the Holy Spirit to work in your lives. It is also not necessary to go around the table or the circle before you move on to the next question. The best discussions are going to occur when everyone feels free to speak during the discussion. The group discussion is actually an opportunity to allow God's Spirit to minister uniquely through one believer to another in very specific ways. Relax and trust God to take the discussion where He wants to take it. If you don't get through all the questions for a session, that's okay.

Concluding Statement and Application

Leave time to read the concluding statement for each session, which will focus the group on application. Application challenges each person to ask, How is my relationship with the Holy Spirit going to be different? We don't want to "merely listen to the word," but we want to "do what it says" (James 1:22). The end game or purpose of the discussion is to help each individual put into practice the things he has learned or discovered in real time. Try to be as specific as possible so you will be able to revisit individual application targets with each individual.

Close Each Session in Prayer

Holy Spirit power comes through prayer. Don't miss out! Reflect on and respond in prayer to what God has revealed or done in the group. Invite the Holy Spirit to continue His work in the ways discussed. Use this time to worship with the Holy Spirit, to be filled, to be convicted, to be healed, and to be motivated by Him. Praying together is the most powerful way to make your discussion effective, meaningful, authentic, and relevant. Do not take it for granted. Instead, lean into it and expect the joy and presence of God to meet you.

Note: Please read chapters 1 and 2 prior to session 1.

session 1: frustration to elevation

Based on chapters 1 and 2 in Soar.

Key Passage: Isaiah 40:28–31

Do you not know? Have you not heard? The LORD is the everlasting God, the Creator of the ends of the earth. He will not grow tired or weary, and his understanding no one can fathom. He gives strength to the weary and increases the power of the weak. Even youths grow tired and weary, and young men stumble and fall; but those who hope in the LORD will renew their strength. They will soar on wings like eagles; they will run and not grow weary, they will walk and not be faint.

Introduction

Two things make men weary and frustrated: the inability to personally change and not being able to catch a break in their circumstances. What many men don't realize is that in the midst of times of change or challenge, personal change and encouragement are available to them through the Holy Spirit. God says that you can turn frustration into elevation by tapping into His power, presence, and process in the midst. Supernaturally, weary and frustrating can morph into energizing and motivating.

Questions

1. What are some changes or challenges that men today are facing that produce fatigue, stress, and fracture in their lives?
2. What is the benefit of having a larger perspective on your life and circumstances?
3. Circle the word you would use to describe your knowledge of and connection to the Holy Spirit. Why?

Intense   **Intimate**   **Occasional**   **Intellectual**   **None**

4. Which of the four **SOAR** principles was most meaningful to you and why?

    Saying yes to the Holy Spirit

    Opening doors of your life to the Holy Spirit

    Actively pursuing the Holy Spirit

    Releasing the power of the Holy Spirit

5. What room of your life would you say has been closed (on purpose or in ignorance) to the work of the Holy Spirit to bring change, freedom, resolution, reconciliation, direction, or healing?

6. Which aspect of personal relationships listed below is most difficult for you? How might this be meaningful to your connection with the Holy Spirit?

    Listening   **Conversing**   **Validating**   **Partnering**

7. Who are some people in your blast zone of influence you would like to impact in a positive way because of the Holy Spirit's power filling you and then exploding out of you to bring the salvation and transformation of God?

The Holy Spirit is an active reality and power. Get that. Low-level living and impact can be replaced with transcendent insight and power in the midst of your right-now life. He is your key to experiencing God's leadership and love, His presence and power, and His purpose and plan. In this study we are on a journey from the place of pride and self-sufficiency to healthy and humble dependency upon the Holy Spirit for leadership. No matter where you are in your walk with God, it is time to go deeper. He's waiting. And, more important, the world is waiting to see, experience, and receive His ministry directly through you as well. It is time to **SOAR.**

To prepare for the next study and discussion, read chapters 3 and 4 of Soar.

session 2: unopened gift

Based on chapters 3 and 4 in Soar.

Key Passage: Acts 2:38

Peter replied, "Repent and be baptized, every one of you, in the name of Jesus Christ for the forgiveness of your sins. And you will receive *the gift* of the Holy Spirit."

Introduction

"I didn't know that!" Game-changing information or intelligence is of little use after the fact. How many times have you said to yourself, "That would have been nice to know"? Finding out after the fact is so deflating, because we could have avoided a lot of pain, experienced a lot more joy, and produced a lot more victories had we known. Many believers are going to feel this way when they get to heaven because they were ignorant of who the Holy Spirit is as well as all the ways He could have helped them in their lives. He was an unopened gift that could have changed everything. But the good news is that it's not too late to get the gift, the help, and the victories.

Questions

1. What thoughts would run through your head if you identified, purchased, and delivered the perfect gift for someone and they chose not to open it or didn't bother using it? What would you say to them?
2. Why do you think God chose to describe the Holy Spirit as a gift? What does He know about us?
3. Why do you think that believers fail to open the gift of a relationship with the Holy Spirit and use Him?
4. What fresh offering of the Holy Spirit do you need today (leadership, revelation, thinking, encouragement, forgiveness, advice, or power to defeat sin)?

5. What issue in your life produces deep fear and requires courage you don't have to address, face, or embrace it?
6. In your community, what would be a giant or evil that pains your heart or boils your blood that needs to be addressed by God's Men?
7. What would be considered shocking behavior on the part of men in your particular culture that would signal to all observers that something powerful was happening among them?
8. As He did with David, where is the Holy Spirit calling you to the front lines spiritually, relationally, or communally when other men are walking away from the giants?

The Holy Spirit prepares us to battle the Goliaths of our lives. God's Men need to bravely respond to the Goliaths He reveals, beginning with personal shortcomings and sin He wants to defeat. The front lines of your relationships, your interactions with people, and their needs are calling while Satan is mocking God's soldiers. It is time to run to battle and rise up. The battle will be won right now in prayer, and your actions will be the cleanup operation. Run to battle in prayer now!

To prepare for the next study and discussion, read chapters 5 and 6 of Soar.

session 3: a good connection

Based on chapters 5 and 6 in Soar.

Key Passage: Psalm 139:23–24

Search me, O God, and know my heart; test me and know my anxious thoughts. See if there is any offensive way in me, and lead me in the way everlasting.

Introduction

Our lives are measured by the quality of our relationships. When people describe a relationship that is going well, they say something like, "Right now we have a good connection." Indirectly, what they are saying is that a disconnecting event or dynamic is being avoided through specific choices. That's the goal of all relationships: learning how to maintain a solid connection with another person. Your spiritual life is measured by the quality of your connection to the Holy Spirit. A good connection means good communication and direction. Disconnection is synonymous with disaster and self-destruction. No-brainer, right?

Questions

1. Which relationships in your life are highly valued and heavily protected to keep the connection healthy and strong? Name some specific benefits of a strong connection to those people.
2. What behaviors or actions do believers engage in that seem innocent from the outside but create real fractures in their relationship with the Holy Spirit and their witness for God?
3. Can you think of a time when you used your connection to God, church, or other Christians for a selfish purpose or to make you look better or appear more acceptable to others?
4. Why do you think the Holy Spirit is grieved when we fail to give grace to others after receiving it from God in Christ?
5. How sensitive are you to the voice of the Holy Spirit? Explain.

   Extremely   **Very**   **Slightly**   **Not at all**

6. When making important decisions, how would you describe yourself?

   Self-Sufficient   **Collaborative**   **God-Dependent**

7. How important is a willing mind to a relationship with God's Spirit?

8. How does knowing that the Holy Spirit wants to be a saving voice in your life help you become a better seeker of His voice and listener to His voice?

The Holy Spirit wants your relationship with Him to be whole, healthy, dynamic, and growing. This means He wants open and honest interaction, responsive relationship, and the authentic closeness those bring. It's a real relationship! Why else would God say, "Don't lie," "Don't grieve," and "Don't put out the Spirit's fire." All are commands, and all are warning signals sent by God to us for our relationship with Him to succeed.

To prepare for the next study and discussion, read chapters 7 and 8 of Soar.

session 4: "now, i see!"

Based on chapters 7 and 8 in Soar.

Key Passage: John 16:13–15

> But when he, the Spirit of truth, comes, he will guide you into all truth. He will not speak on his own; he will speak only what he hears, and he will tell you what is yet to come. He will bring glory to me by taking from what is mine and making it known to you. All that belongs to the Father is mine. That is why I said the Spirit will take from what is mine and make it known to you.

Introduction

It feels almost magical. They are referred to as aha! moments. We shout the words, whisper them to ourselves, think them, or just take a deep breath and smile. Something that has been eluding us either dawns on us or comes into clear view. We all know the feeling. Jesus said that the Holy Spirit would provide every believer with insight into God's mind on all things. He is the aha behind all aha's, and His goal is to provide a new set of eyes with which to see God, self, and life. God changes the way we perceive reality by helping us to filter and look at everything from His perspective. Especially, He changes how we love.

Questions

1. What are a few of the most profound realizations you have ever had? (For example, a discovery of truth that has deeply impacted or changed the way you approach life.)
2. Why is it important to distinguish between your perception or opinion on an issue and God's revelation on an issue?
3. What is the connection between the Holy Spirit living within you and your ability to discern God's will?
4. How do you know if someone is listening consistently to the Holy Spirit in his life?
5. Why do you think helping believers heal relationships and love better is the most important work the Holy Spirit does?
6. What is the connection between being set free by the Holy Spirit and being able to love others freely?
7. Who is the Holy Spirit calling you to love sacrificially? What help or insight do you need from Him to pull it off?

The Holy Spirit wants to donate God's wisdom and insight to you so that you can perceive and process reality differently. He does this in various ways, beginning with the revelation of Jesus Christ Himself, progressively revealing more and more about God to us through God's Word or speaking directly to our minds. Just like Mike May's dramatic journey from blindness to eyesight, the Holy Spirit is seeking to regenerate and heal all diseased thinking and replace it with His discernment and insight. The Bible promises the mind of Christ to those who "keep in step with the Spirit" (Galatians 5:25). His aha's are going to rock your world and help you connect with others in your life in a deeper, more powerful and effective way—if you let Him.

To prepare for the next study and discussion, read chapters 9, 10, and 11 of Soar.

session 5: an attitude of gratitude

Based on chapters 9, 10, and 11 in Soar.

Key Passage: Romans 14:17–18

For the kingdom of God is not a matter of eating and drinking, but of righteousness, peace and joy in the Holy Spirit, because anyone who serves Christ
in this way is pleasing to God and approved by men.

Introduction

After our salvation, the Holy Spirit immediately throws into gear the process of
making us more and more like Jesus. First, He does this by calling us to be men,
not boys. He starts out by kneading the love of God into every area of our bondage
and pain, thus creating a new security in our soul. Then He spreads that healing
and the freedom we are experiencing into our relationships with others. The Holy
Spirit also sets us free from the slavery of seeking our fulfillment in sources other
than God by teaching us to accept, be grateful for, and to live contently in the life
God has given us.

Questions

1. Why does it seem so difficult for some men to grow up? to stop being a boy and
   become a man?
2. Why is it that God often uses the experience of a broken heart to accomplish
   important spiritual progress in our life?
3. What are some of the "if only" situations (see page 112) in your life that may be
   keeping you from accepting God's plans for you?
4. Why is faithfulness so important in overcoming feelings when a man faces a
   temptation or other challenge?

5. Why are gratitude and contentment such important qualities for a Christian?

6. Why is reading and meditating on God's Word so important to the man who wants to live a life of discipline and purpose?

7. In what areas of your life do you need to wake up so you can better follow the Holy Spirit's direction and enter into battle?

8. What blessings from God are you most thankful for?

When we are filled with, cooperating with, and learning truth from the Holy Spirit, we have the ability and power to turn away from foolish, boyish ways and become authentic God's Men. When a man is able to stop going in one direction and say, "I don't have to have that, I don't have to do that, I don't have to say that, I don't have to think that, I don't have to eat that, I don't have to drink that, I don't have to click that, I don't have to see that, I don't have to touch that, I don't have to buy that, I don't have to listen to that," he is growing into all aspects in Christ through the power and process of the Holy Spirit in his life. At that point, he can truly know that "godliness with contentment is great gain" (1 Timothy 6:6).

To prepare for the next study and discussion, read chapters 12 and 13 of Soar.

session 6: blast zone

Based on chapters 12 and 13 in Soar.

Key Passage: Luke 4:18–19

The Spirit of the Lord is on me, because he has anointed me to preach good news to the poor. He has sent me to proclaim freedom for the prisoners and recovery of sight for the blind, to release the oppressed, to proclaim the year of the Lord's favor.

Introduction

God's Men, for better or for worse, have been given the ability to produce life and death through their character and conduct. Like the men who were a part of the first massive explosion of the Spirit at Pentecost, we have the opportunity to leave our "Egypts" behind, let God change us, and rock our world for God. We are not asked to do anything beyond what the Holy Spirit has given us the character, courage, gifts, and power to accomplish. Something amazing is bubbling inside us, and it's just a matter of time before it erupts. God has big plans for His men. The world is waiting!

Questions

1. Why might it be true that so many of the social problems in the world today are a result of broken male leadership?
2. What are some examples of an Egypt in a man's life—some things in his character, morals, behavior—that need to be left behind?
3. What are some Egypts you have faced in your life?
4. What areas of your life might benefit most from the power of the Holy Spirit?
5. Why is the Holy Spirit never deposited inside of a man for the sole purpose of remaining there?
6. What is a man's "blast zone of influence"? What is yours?
7. Why do you think God has such a tender heart toward people who are marginalized by society?
8. What people in your life need the deliverance from bondage to freedom that only the Holy Spirit can accomplish?

The Holy Spirit has designs on our moment in time and wants to work through us in culturally powerful ways to make a difference. The book of Acts is still being written, and we're part of it! The Holy Spirit has not changed His ways. All the gifts of the Holy Spirit are still available, and He allocates them to us as He chooses, just as He did with the first disciples in their blast zones of influence. We have been shaped uniquely for impact in our context today, and it's our responsibility to determine what spiritual gifts the Holy Spirit has given us to help change our world for God's glory.

To prepare for the next study and discussion, read chapters 14 and 15 of Soar.

session 7: help lift a burden

Based on chapters 14 and 15 in Soar.

Key Passage: Matthew 11:28–30, NLT

Then Jesus said, "Come to me, all of you who are weary and carry heavy burdens, and I will give you rest. Take my yoke upon you. Let me teach you, because I am humble and gentle at heart, and you will find rest for your souls. For my yoke is easy to bear, and the burden I give you is light."

Introduction

Jesus regularly stood up for the vulnerable, stigmatized, and isolated to make them feel accepted by God, secure in His presence, and affirmed as people worthy of salvation. The ethnically, morally, physically, and culturally unacceptable were all deemed acceptable by Jesus. Those normally kept *out* had an *in* with Him. And they loved Jesus for it! Lepers, prostitutes, Samaritans, tax collectors, gluttons, children, women, the diseased, crippled, mentally unstable, and all manner of sinners were at home with Jesus. Working seamlessly with the Holy Spirit, Jesus fully expressed the heart of God toward these aliens in His own culture. He challenged His disciples—then and now—to follow in His steps.

Questions

1. How is your response to challenges in your life changed by knowing that Jesus has lifted your personal load of guilt and sin?

2. By your own definition, what does it mean to live for an audience of one?

3. How is the Holy Spirit the Helper in your life?

4. What would you list as the first-mile responsibilities in your life? What are some examples of second-mile responsibilities?

5. In the first century, the men of Pentecost overcame many cultural and religious barriers. What might be some barriers today that the Holy Spirit wants God's Men to overcome?

6. Who might be examples of the poorest in spirit in your daily life?

7. In your group, take turns sharing some stories of how you have lifted the burden in the life of another person. How did helping out make you feel?

8. Ask the Holy Spirit to bring to your mind one or two individuals who you could surprise by showing up and saying, "How can I help you?"

The mission of the Holy Spirit in us is to make God real to others by unburdening them in unexpected ways. Unexpected, because they are used to seeing and experiencing so much selfishness in others. At a moment's notice, God's Men who are filled with the Holy Spirit are called to abandon agendas, rights, offended feelings, and resentments to lighten another's load. This is what Jesus did, as did the men of Pentecost. It's what we need to do today. Spirit-filled men end up doing things they never imagined in order to create a witness of His work in and through them.

To prepare for the next study and discussion, read chapters 16 and 17 of Soar.

session 8: a special assignment

Based on chapters 16 and 17 in Soar.

Key Passage: Luke 15:4

Suppose one of you has a hundred sheep and loses one of them. Does he not leave the ninety-nine in the open country and go after the lost sheep until he finds it?

Introduction

The Holy Spirit equips us for two important and meaningful ministries in the lives of others. With our Jesus-following brothers and sisters, we have the opportunity to encourage them in their walk with God. With those who are not yet followers of Jesus, we have the exciting opportunity (under the guidance and direction of the Holy Spirit) of prayerfully, thoughtfully, and intentionally sharing the good news of God's plan to redeem mankind from the futility of spiritual darkness and death. Those two critical assignments in the kingdom of God should stir the blood of every God's Man!

Questions

1. How did God the Father encourage Jesus?
2. What are some ways that we can edify other believers?
3. Why is being a good listener so important in offering encouragement to another person?
4. Share some personal examples of how others have given you encouragement. What was the result in your life?
5. Why, as Kenny writes, is evangelism synonymous with inconvenience?
6. In regard to sharing the gospel, how do you think you might exchange fear for freedom?
7. If "every man is a missionary," what would you say is your mission field?
8. To wrap up our discussion: Of the things you have learned, what stands out in your mind? What prayer requests do you have as you move forward with the Holy Spirit to represent Christ to the world?

Every one of us is a missionary who will make a mark on the world. We do this by being Jesus in our blast zone of influence. Encouraging our brothers and sisters, relieving someone's pain, reducing someone's load, raising someone's spirit, and reaching someone's soul is how the Holy Spirit gets the job done through us. We can't do it without His help and power. Only a proud fool would try! The journey from fear to freedom in our personal mission for God on earth depends on one person: the Holy Spirit. Are you ready to accept His friendship, wisdom, and power and then go?

notes

1. Chin Saik Yoon, "Phone call saved scores of Indian villagers from tsunami," December 2004, www.idrc.ca/panasia/ev-68766-201-1-DO_TOPIC.html.
2. The entire story of this incredible, risk-filled journey from blindness to sight is recounted in Robert Kurson, *Crashing Through: A True Story of Risk, Adventure, and the Man Who Dared to See* (New York: Random House, 2008).
3. C. S. Lewis, *Letters of C. S. Lewis,* ed. W. H. Lewis (New York: Harcourt, Brace & World, 1966), 256.
4. George Pararas-Carayannis, "The Great Explosion of the Krakatau Volcano ("Krakatoa") of August 26, 1883, in Indonesia," The Tsunami Page of Dr. George P.C., www.drgeorgepc.com/Volcano1883Krakatoa.html.

about the author

Kenny Luck is the men's pastor at Saddleback Church in Lake Forest, California, where over 7,000 men are connected in small groups. He is also the founder and president of Every Man Ministries, which helps churches worldwide develop and grow healthy men's communities.

He is an ECPA Platinum Award–winning author who has authored and coauthored over 18 books, including *Dream; Risk; Fight; Every Man, God's Man; Every Young Man, God's Man;* and the *Every Man Bible Studies* from the best-selling Every Man Series published by WaterBrook Press/Random House. Kenny has made numerous radio and television appearances as an expert on men's issues including ABC Family, Christian Broadcasting Network, and over 100 other radio and television programs worldwide. He has been a featured contributor to Rick Warren's *Ministry Toolbox, New Man* magazine, *Men of Integrity, The Journal,* and *Young Believer* magazine.

Kenny is a graduate of UCLA, where he met his wife, Chrissy. They have three children, Cara, Ryan, and Jenna, and live in Trabuco Canyon, California.

For more information, contact:
Every Man Ministries
(949) 609-8780
www.everymanministries.com

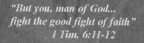

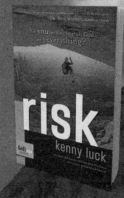

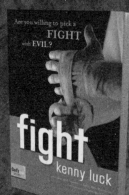
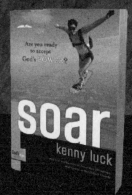